A STATA COMPANION FOR *THE FUNDAMENTALS OF SOCIAL RESEARCH*

A Stata Companion for The Fundamentals of Social Research offers students the opportunity to delve into the world of Stata using real data sets and statistical analysis techniques directly from Paul M. Kellstedt, Guy D. Whitten, and Steven A. Tuch's new textbook. Workbook sections parallel chapters in the main text, giving students a chance to apply the lessons and techniques learned in each chapter in a statistical software setting. Detailed chapters teach students to reproduce results presented in the textbook, allowing them to become comfortable performing statistical analyses for evaluating causal claims through repeated practice. Step-by-step instructions for using Stata are provided, along with command lines and screenshots to demonstrate proper use of the software. Instructions for producing the figures and tables in the main text are integrated throughout the workbook. End-of-chapter exercises encourage students to formulate and evaluate their own hypotheses.

Paul M. Kellstedt is a professor of political science at Texas A&M University.

Guy D. Whitten is a professor of political science and Director of the European Union Center at Texas A&M University.

Steven A. Tuch is a professor of sociology and public policy and public administration at George Washington University.

A STATA COMPANION FOR

The Fundamentals of Social Research

Paul M. Kellstedt

Texas A&M University

Guy D. Whitten

Texas A&M University

Steven A. Tuch

George Washington University

CAMBRIDGE
UNIVERSITY PRESS

CAMBRIDGE
UNIVERSITY PRESS

University Printing House, Cambridge CB2 8BS, United Kingdom

One Liberty Plaza, 20th Floor, New York, NY 10006, USA

477 Williamstown Road, Port Melbourne, VIC 3207, Australia

314–321, 3rd Floor, Plot 3, Splendor Forum, Jasola District Centre,
New Delhi – 110025, India

103 Penang Road, #05–06/07, Visioncrest Commercial, Singapore 238467

Cambridge University Press is part of the University of Cambridge.

It furthers the University's mission by disseminating knowledge in the pursuit of
education, learning, and research at the highest international levels of excellence.

www.cambridge.org
Information on this title: www.cambridge.org/highereducation/isbn/9781009248242
DOI: 10.1017/9781009248259

First published 2023

A catalogue record for this publication is available from the British Library.

ISBN 978-1-009-24824-2 Paperback

Brief Contents

Contents

Figures

Preface

This software companion book represents an effort to provide both extra exercises, as well as hands-on material for how to put the techniques that we discuss in *The Fundamentals of Social Research* into action. It is one of three workbooks, each written to help students to work with the materials covered in *The Fundamentals of Social Research* using a particular piece of statistical software.

This workbook focuses on using the program Stata. (The other companion books are designed to work with SPSS and R.) Our expectation is that the typical user of this book will be using a relatively recent version of Stata on a computer that is running some version of the Windows operating system. We also have made an effort to accommodate users who are using some version of macOS or OS X. An online appendix available at www.cambridge.org/fsr will help Mac users with any difficulties.

The chapter structure of this workbook mirrors the chapter structure of *The Fundamentals of Social Research*. We have written with the expectation that students will read the chapters of this companion after they have read the chapters of the book.

We continue to update both the general and instructor-only sections of the webpage for our book (www.cambridge.org/fsr). As before, the general section contains data sets available in formats compatible with SPSS, Stata, and R. The instructor-only section contains several additional resources, including PowerPoint and TEX/Beamer slides for each chapter, a test-bank, and answer keys for the exercises.

1 The Scientific Study of Society

1.1 OVERVIEW

In this chapter we introduce you to some of the important building blocks of a scientific approach to studying the social world. As you can already tell from reading the first chapter of *The Fundamentals of Social Research* – which we will refer to as "*FSR*" or the "main text" from here on – data are an important part of what we do both to explore the world and to test hypotheses based on causal theories. An important part of working with data is learning how to use a statistical software package. In the sections that follow, we introduce you to the Stata program and some basics that you will need to get up and running. In doing this, we also introduce some general principles of good computing practices for effectively working with data.

1.2 "A WORKBOOK? WHY IS THERE A WORKBOOK?"

You might be asking yourself this question, and it's perfectly fair to do so. Allow us to try to explain how this workbook fits in with the main *FSR* text.

As you will see in the weeks and months to follow in your class, the main textbook will teach you about the use of statistics in the social sciences, mostly by using equations and examples. So yes, in some ways, it will feel rather math-y. (And we think that's cool, though we realize that it's not everyone's cup of tea.) One of the ways that people learn about the practice of statistics is to use computer software to calculate statistics directly. To that end, many instructors want students to learn to use a particular computer software package so they can begin to conduct statistical analyses themselves.[1] We have discovered through years

---

[1] This particular software companion book teaches students to use Stata, but we have also produced parallel books for instructors who wish to have their students learn SPSS or R.

of teaching that this transition between equations in a book and software output on a computer screen is a very difficult one. The goal of this software companion book is to make this connection stronger, even seamless.

If we are successful, this book will do two things. First, it will teach the nuts and bolts about how to use Stata. Though many (perhaps most) students today are quite computer-literate, we believe that having a reference guide for students to learn the techniques, or for them to teach themselves out of class time, will be helpful. Second, and more importantly, this software guide will provide explicit hand-holding to you as you learn to connect the key principles from the main text to the practical issues of producing and interpreting statistical results.

Each chapter of this software guide works in parallel with that of the main *FSR* text. So when you learn the equations of two-variable regression analysis in Chapter 10 of the main text, you will learn the details about using Stata to estimate two-variable regression models in Chapter 10 of this companion book. And so on. In the end, we hope that the very important (but perhaps rather abstract) equations in the text become more meaningful to you as you learn to estimate the statistics yourself, and then to learn to interpret them meaningfully and clearly. Those three things – formulae, software, and interpretation – together provide a very solid foundation and basic understanding of social science.

Let's start.

1.3 GETTING STARTED WITH STATA

To get started with Stata, we recommend that you set yourself up in front of a computer that has the program installed with a copy of *FSR* close by. You should also have the set of computer files that accompany this text (which you can download from the text's website, www.cambridge.org/fsr) in a directory on the computer on which you are working. You will get the most out of this workbook by working in Stata as you read this workbook.

The instructions in this book can help you learn Stata whether you use a Windows-based PC or a Mac. Once the program is launched, Stata works identically, no matter which platform you use. Mac users should be aware, though, that our screenshots will come from a Windows-based PC. Some of those screenshots that involve finding and opening files on your computer, therefore, will look somewhat unfamiliar to Mac users, but we assume that Mac users are at least somewhat used to this. Overall, the differences between running Stata on Windows compared to a Mac are minimal. That said, we have created a help guide on the differences between working with Stata on a Windows-based PC and a Mac operating system, which can be found online at www.cambridge.org/fsr.

Finally, we wrote this book while using versions 16 and 17 of Stata. Particularly for the statistical fundamentals you will learn in this book, the differences between versions – at least as old as Stata 12 – are not severe. In fact, if you use any version of Stata between 12 and 17, you might not notice the difference between what appears on your screen and what appears in the screenshots contained in this book.

1.3.1 Launching Stata

When you are sitting in front of a computer on which Stata has been properly installed, you can launch the program by double-clicking on the Stata icon or by finding the Stata program on your start menu. Once you have successfully launched the Stata program, you will sometimes be prompted with a small box of options for updating the program like what we see in Figure 1.1. If this box does pop up when you launch the program, then we recommend that, for now, you click the option "Check next time Stata is launched" and then click "OK."

At this point, you should see one large window like that in Figure 1.2. Within this main Stata window, you will see four other windows labeled "History" (on the left side), "Variables" (on the top right side), "Properties" (on the bottom right side) and "Command" (across the bottom). The remaining area in the middle, known as the "Results" window, is not labeled. If you are seeing all of this, you are ready to go.

1.3.2 Getting Stata to Do Things

In almost any mainstream statistical program today, there are multiple ways to accomplish the same tasks. In Stata, almost any command can be executed using pull-down menus, typed commands in the command window, or typed commands in a do-file window. The choice of which

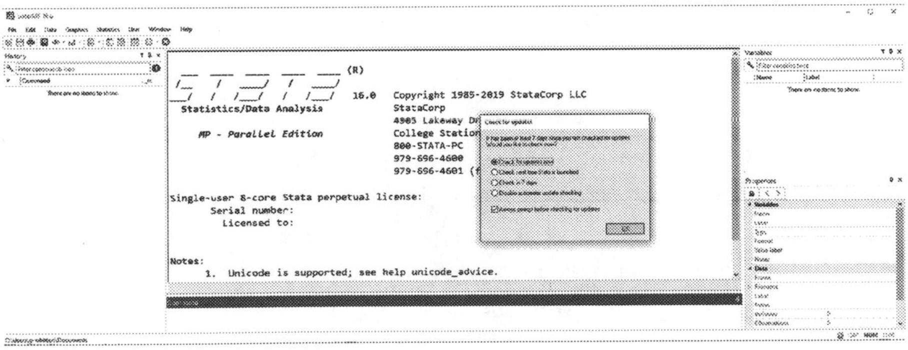

Figure 1.1 Stata after initial launch with update options box

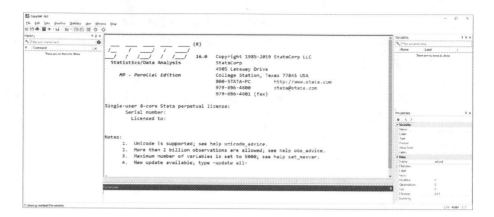

Figure 1.2 Stata initial launch

of these options to use is a matter of personal comfort. But, as we discuss below, no matter which way you choose to get Stata to do things, you need to keep track of what you are doing. We now discuss the three ways to get Stata to do things by showing an example of opening a data set. We recommend that you try all three, but especially the example of using a do-file in the final subsection below.

Using Pull-Down Menus

If you prefer to use pull-down menus, you need to start with either the row of textual headings across the top left of the program (starting with "File," then "Edit," etc.) or, immediately under that, the row of icons (a picture of a folder opening, a picture of a floppy disk, etc.). In our initial example, we are going to open a data set, so we need to start either with the textual heading "File" or with the icon that looks like a folder being opened. In Figure 1.3, we show what this will look like if we click on "File."

Once you have clicked on "File," you will want to direct Stata to the location on your computer where you have placed the *FSR* Stata companion files (as we noted above, these can be downloaded from www .cambridge.org/fsr). In our running example, these files are located in the directory "C:\MyFSRStataFiles." So, to find our initial data set, named "African American Home Ownership 1985-2014", we would point Stata to this directory and then click on the file "African American Home Ownership 1985-2014" as shown in Figure 1.4.

Once you have done this correctly, your Stata screen should look like Figure 1.5. A few things have changed:

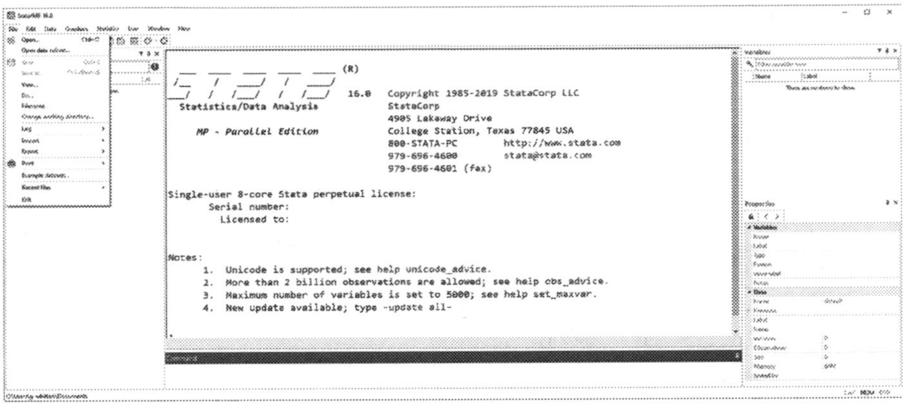

Figure 1.3 Stata with pull-down menu for "File" selected

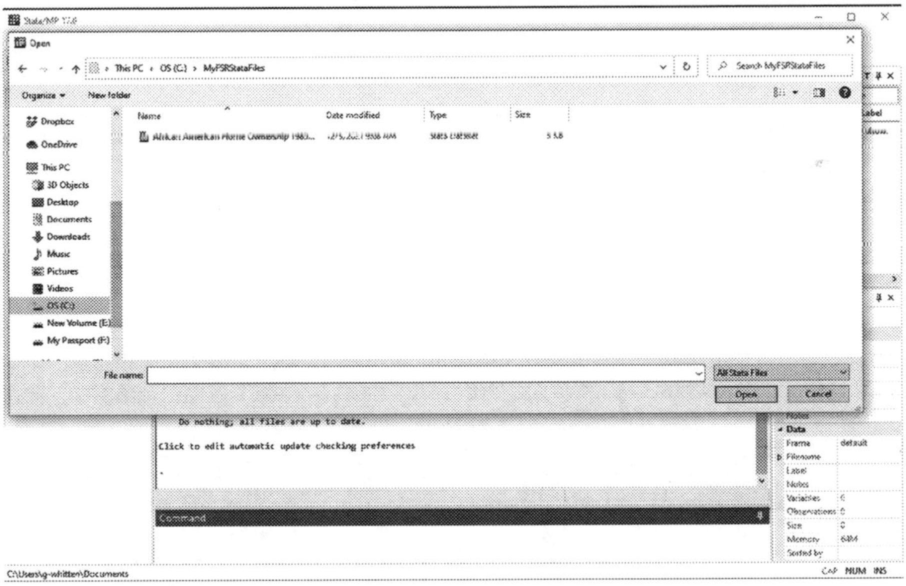

Figure 1.4 Stata with directory open

- In the "Results" window, we can see the text

  `. use "C:\MyFSRStataFiles\African American Home Ownership 1985-2014.dta"`

  where

  – the "." in front of this line indicates that this is a command that Stata has executed,

  – the name of the command is "use" which is the main Stata command for accessing a data set,

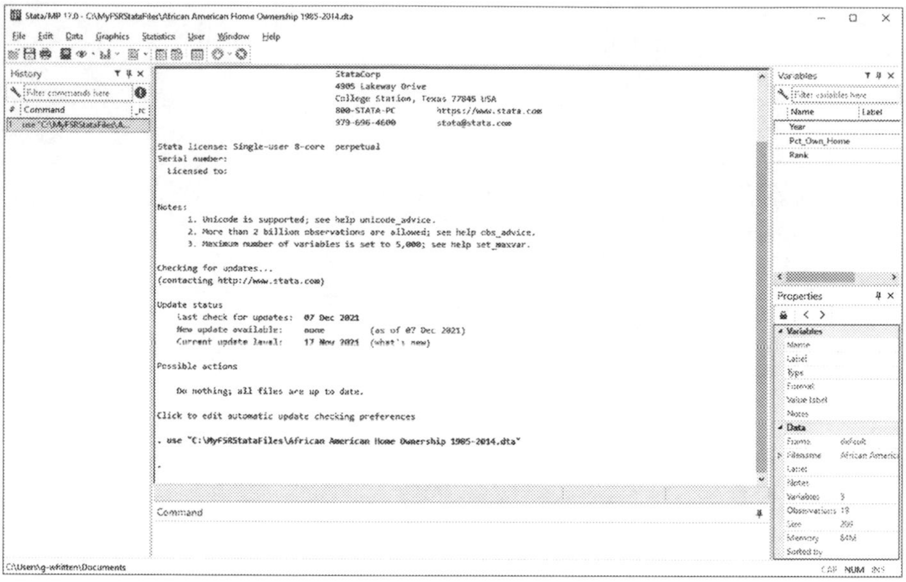

Figure 1.5 Stata with data loaded in

- the text in quotes tells us the name of the file and location where the file was obtained.

- In the upper left corner, at the top of the "History" window, we see the number 1 in the "#" column followed by the beginning of the text of the command. This is where Stata keeps track of each command that it has executed.
- On the right side, we can see that there is new information in the "Variables" and "Properties" windows.

  - In the "Variables" window, we can see the names of the three variables that are contained in this data set.
  - In the "Properties" window, we can see some information about each variable and some information about the data set. In particular, we can tell that the data set contains three variables and nineteen observations.

Using the Command Window

You can type commands directly into the command window that you see across the bottom of the initial window that opens when you launch the program. These commands are typed in one at a time, and are executed by the program when you hit the "Enter" button on your keyboard.

So, if we want to load the data set "African American Home Ownership 1985-2014," which is a Stata data set (with the ".dta" suffix), you would type the following command into the "Command" window and hit the "Enter" key on your computer:

```
use "C:\MyFSRStataFiles\African American Home Ownership
1985-2014.dta", clear
```

If you have done this correctly, your Stata will look like Figure 1.5, except that it will have the ", clear" at the end.[2] The ", clear" tells us that Stata cleared out any data that we had sitting in the program's memory before it opened our data set.

Using a Do-File

A third way to issue commands in Stata is to use a do-file. While this method of working will seem a little bit clumsy at first, it is our preferred method of working in Stata for reasons that we will explain below. To work with a do-file, you need to open a new window called a "Do-file Editor." To do this, go to the pull-down menus on the top left of the program and select "Window," "Do-file Editor," and finally left-click on "New Do-file Editor," as shown in Figure 1.6. We will eventually cover a lot of different things that one can do with a do-file, but, for now, all that we want you to do is to type the following command into the new do-file:

```
use "C:\MyFSRStataFiles\African American Home Ownership
1985-2014.dta", clear
```

Once you have typed this command into the do-file editor, you will then want to select the entire line – you can do this by left-clicking at the beginning of the line and then moving to the end and releasing the left mouse button – and then click on the icon at the right side of the top of the do-file window that looks like a piece of paper with writing on it with an arrow pointing to the right in the lower right corner of the icon. Clicking on this icon, named "Execute Selection (do)," will tell the program to execute the selected line of code. In Figure 1.7, we show what this will look like right before you click on "Execute Selection (do)." Once you have done this correctly, you will see output in the main window that looks like Figure 1.5.

---

[2] The location of files is often a stumbling block for beginning users of a statistical software package. To keep things simple, we recommend that you create a folder on your computer's C drive named "MyFSRStataFiles" and put all of the files that you have downloaded from www.cambridge.org/fsr into that folder. If you are unable to do this, then on a computer using a Windows operating system you can find the exact name of the location of a file by right-clicking on that file, left-clicking "Properties," and then looking at the entry to the right of "Location." This filepath, or location, can be selected, copied, and pasted directly into your command window (or do-file) to ensure that it is exactly right. As discussed earlier, a help guide on the differences between working on a Windows-based PC and a Mac operating system can be found online at www.cambridge.org/fsr.

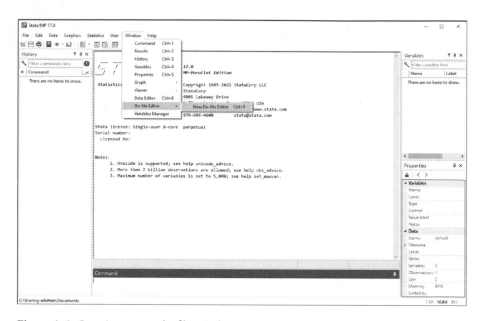

Figure 1.6 Opening a new do-file window

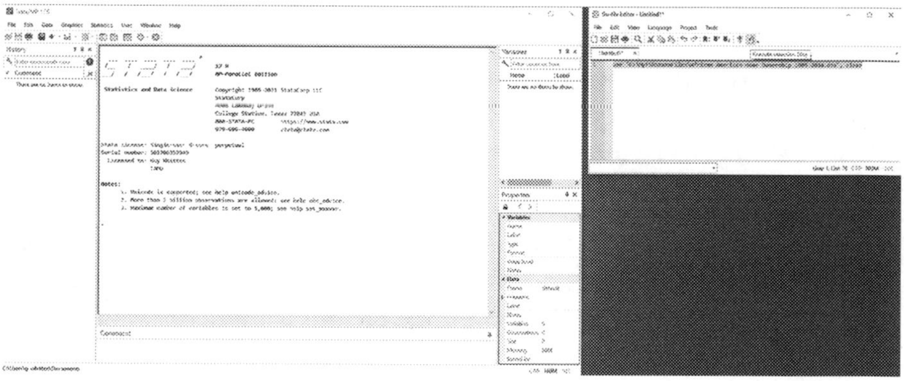

Figure 1.7 Executing a command from a do-file editor

1.3.3   Initially Examining Data in Stata

Now that we have shown you three different ways to get a data set into Stata, we want you to take a look at the data that you have loaded into the program.[3] These data are from the 1985–2014 General Social Surveys (GSSs), a data set that you will become quite familiar with in your statistics course because we make extensive use of it in this workbook as well as in the main text. The particular survey question that we examine in this

---

[3] We discuss how to manually enter your own data into a Stata file in an online appendix, available at www.cambridge.org/fsr.

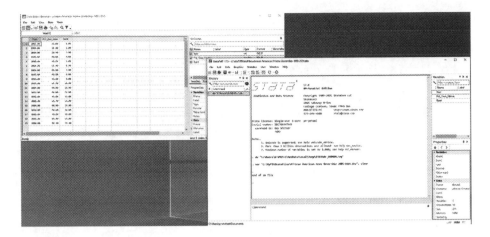

Figure 1.8 Initially examining data in Stata

illustration asks respondents whether they own or rent the dwelling in which they currently live. To get an initial look at these data, click on the "Data Editor (Browse)" icon which can be found in the top left of the main Stata window – it is the icon that looks like a spreadsheet with a magnifying glass over it. Once you have done this, your computer should look something like Figure 1.8. Each column in this spreadsheet contains values for a single variable and each row contains data from a single election.

In Figure 1.8, you will see data in three columns, labeled from left to right as "Year," "Pct_Own_Home," and "Rank." Those labels correspond to the names of the three variables in our data set. Down the rows you will see the cases of the three variables. For example, in row 10 of the data window, which is the tenth case in the data set, we see the following values for the three variables. "Year" takes on the value of 1993, "Pct_Own_Home" has the value of 43.90, and "Rank" has the value 10.00. These variable names make clear what each variable represents and what the corresponding values mean.

You can use the bars at the right and at the bottom of the data set to scroll through it. As you already know, this data set has only three variables, so you need to scroll to the right to see any other variables. However, you can use the bar at the right of the screen to scroll down when you have larger data sets. For now, you'll notice that the last of our cases has a value for "Year" of 1990 and a value for "Pct_Own_Home" of 54.90. You can also see that the data set has a total of nineteen cases.

You are now ready to proceed to the end-of-chapter exercises.

EXERCISES

1. Go through all of the steps described above. Once you have the "Data View" open (so that your computer looks like Figure 1.8), do the following:

   (a) Look at the values in the column labeled "Pct_Own_Home." This is our measure of homeownership. Do the following:

      i. Identify the year with the highest value for this variable.

      ii. Identify the year with the lowest value for this variable.

      iii. What does it mean if this variable goes up by one?

   (b) Look at the values in the column labeled "Rank." This is our measure of the rank, from lowest to highest, of the proportion of African American homeownership in the years from 1985 to 2014. Now do the following:

      i. Identify the year with the highest value for this variable.

      ii. Identify the year with the lowest value for this variable.

      iii. What does it mean if this variable goes up by one?

2 The Art of Theory Building

2.1 OVERVIEW

One of our emphases in *FSR* has been on producing new causal theories, and then evaluating whether or not those theories are supported by evidence. In this chapter, we describe how to explore sources of variation – both across space, and across time – to get you started thinking about new explanations for interesting phenomena. We also help you explore how new theories can be built upon the existing work in the literature.

2.2 EXAMINING VARIATION ACROSS TIME AND ACROSS SPACE

As we discuss in Section 2.3 of *FSR*, one way to develop ideas about causal theories is to identify interesting variation. In that section, we discuss examining two types of variation, cross-sectional and time-series variation. In this section, we show you how to create figures like the ones presented in Section 2.3 of *FSR*. Although there are many different types of graphs that can be used to examine variation in variables, we recommend a bar graph for cross-sectional variation and a connected plot for time-series variation.

As you will see from these examples, Stata's graph commands can often be quite long because of all of the options that we typically like to include. We therefore recommend that you start with the main command and then add the options until you get a figure that looks right to you. For the example of the bar graph, we go through these steps in some detail.

2.2.1 Producing a Bar Graph for Examining Cross-Sectional Variation

A useful way to get a sense of the variation for a cross-sectional variable is to produce a bar graph in which you display the values of that variable across spatial units. In the example that we display in Figure 2.2 of *FSR*, we have a bar graph of Gini coefficients in 2013 for twenty-three randomly

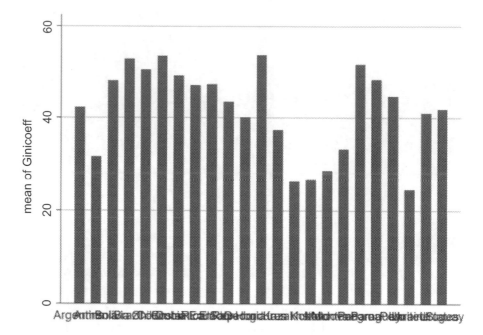

Figure 2.1 Initial bar graph of Gini coefficients

selected nations. Building on what we learned in Chapter 1, we will now show you how to produce a figure like this in Stata. The first step to doing this is the command:

```
use "C:\MyFSRStataFiles\Gini_Coefficients_2013.dta", clear
```

which will load the appropriate data set into Stata. Once you have this data set properly loaded into Stata, you will want to issue a command to produce a bar graph of the variable GiniCoeff for each spatial unit. In this case, the spatial unit is Country. So the command for producing such a bar graph is:

```
graph bar GiniCoeff, over(Country)
```

where "graph bar" tells Stata that we want to produce a bar graph. The next part of the command, "GiniCoeff," is the name of the variable whose values we want to graph. By default, commands in Stata are written on a single line and submitted to the program. We can break each command into the main part of the command and then the optional part of the command. The optional part is the text that follows a comma. So, for this command the option that we have chosen with ", over(Country)" tells the program that we want to have a bar graph across the values of Country. We can see the results from submitting this command in Figure 2.1. Although we have the values of "GiniCoeff" displayed in a bar graph, we are unable to read names of the nations for which

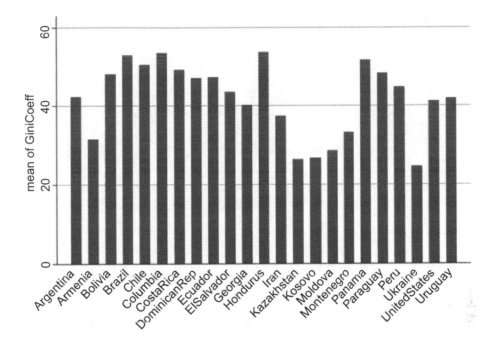

Figure 2.2 Initial bar graph of Gini coefficients with angled labels

these values are displayed. This is because they have all been displayed horizontally under each bar and they run into each other. To fix this, we can add a further option to our command by typing

```
graph bar GiniCoeff, over(Country, label(angle(45)))
```

where ", label(angle(45))" tells Stata that we want the labels displayed at a forty-five degree angle. The result from this command is displayed in Figure 2.2.

Compare Figure 2.2 here with Figure 2.2 in *FSR*. What is the difference between these two figures? The answer is that in Figure 2.2 in *FSR* the values of the Gini coefficients have been sorted from smallest to largest. When displaying data in graphs, it is important that you do so in a fashion that allows you and your readers to most easily make the assessments that they want to make. In this case, since we are trying to think about what makes a country spend more or less of its GDP on its military, we want to be able to see which countries spend more or less. Try comparing the value of Gini coefficients between Argentina and El Salvador in the graph that we just made, Figure 2.2. Not an easy thing to do! It's a lot easier using Figure 2.2 from *FSR* because the cases have been *sorted*. You might have also noticed that the label on the vertical axis in Figure 2.2 is more communicative. We can make these two adjustments by writing the command

```
graph bar GiniCoeff, /*
*/ , over(Country, label(angle(45)) sort(GiniCoeff)) /*
*/ scheme(s1mono) /*
*/ ytitle("2013 Gini coefficients")
```

where "sort(GiniCoeff)" tells Stata to sort the bars by the values of "GiniCoeff" and "ytitle("2013 Gini coefficients")" tells Stata to insert a more informative label on the *y* axis. There are two additional elements of this command that need to be explained. First, you will have probably noticed that this command now takes up four lines with each line except for the first started with a */ and each line except for the last ended with a /*. We have done this because Stata reads each line as a new command. When Stata encounters a /*, it ignores everything until it sees a */. Thus Stata reads the four lines of code that we have written above as though they were strung together as one single line of code. One alternative would be for us to have written all four lines above as one single long line. But the problem with this alternative is that it would be difficult for us to keep track of. And, second, you will probably have noticed the option "scheme(s1mono)" on the third line of this command. This tells Stata that we want the graph to be drawn using the graphics scheme named "s1mono." The different graphics schemes in Stata determine the overall look of the figures that Stata produces. You can find out more about these by issuing the command help graph scheme and then left-clicking on the blue text "schemes intro."

All of the commands for this example are contained in a do-file called "Chapter 2 Bar Graph Example.do" which can be found in the MyFSRStataFiles directory.

2.2.2 Producing a Connected Plot for Examining Time-Series Variation

A useful way to get a sense of the variation for a time-series variable is to produce a connected plot in which you display the values of that variable *connected* across time. In the example that we display in Figure 2.1 of *FSR*, we have a connected plot of the values for U.S. presidential approval each month from February 1995 to December 2005. Building on what we learned in Chapter 1, we will now show you how to produce a figure like this in Stata. As with the previous example, the first step to doing this is to run the command:

```
use "C:\MyFSRStataFiles\presap9505.dta", clear
```

which loads the data. The command for producing Figure 2.1 of *FSR* is

```
graph twoway connected presap year_month , /*
*/ xlabel(420(6)540, angle(45)) ytitle("Presidential
Approval") /*
*/ xtitle("Year/Month") legend(off) scheme(s1mono)
```

where

- "graph twoway connected" tells Stata that we want to produce a graph from the "twoway" set of graphs[1] and that the specific type of twoway graph that we want is a "connected" graph,[2]
- "presap" and "year" are the variables that will define the vertical and horizontal dimensions of the graph,
- the comma after "year" indicates the start of the options part of the command,
- "xlabel(420(6)540, angle(45))" tells Stata that we want to label the time points from time point 420 to 540 with labels every six points[3] and that, as we did in the previous section, we want labels to appear at a forty-five degree angle,
- "ytitle("Presidential Approval")" and "xtitle("Year/Month")" tell Stata the variable labels for the vertical and horizontal axes,
- "legend(off)" tells Stata that we do not want a legend box to appear at the bottom of our graph, and
- "scheme(s1mono)" tells Stata that we want to graph to be produced using the scheme "s1mono."

All of the commands for this example are contained in a do-file called "Chapter 2 Connected Graph Example.do" which can be found in the MyFSRStataFiles directory.

2.3 USING GOOGLE SCHOLAR TO SEARCH THE LITERATURE EFFECTIVELY

We assume that you're skilled at web searches, likely using Google's search engine. In addition to the myriad other things that Google allows us to

---

[1] As we will see in later chapters, Stata has a large number of different twoway graphs.

[2] A connected graph is one in which a circle represents each observation and then these circles are connected together by lines.

[3] Stata has a particular way of dealing with time-series data. Time-series dates are given unique identifying values. In the case of Stata's conventions for dealing with monthly data, such as those in this example, January 1960 is assigned the unique identifying value of 0. This means that January 1995 is assigned the value 420 and December 540. Although our data begin in February of 1995, we decided to start the display of the months on the horizontal dimension of Figure 2.2 in *FSR* in January 1995.

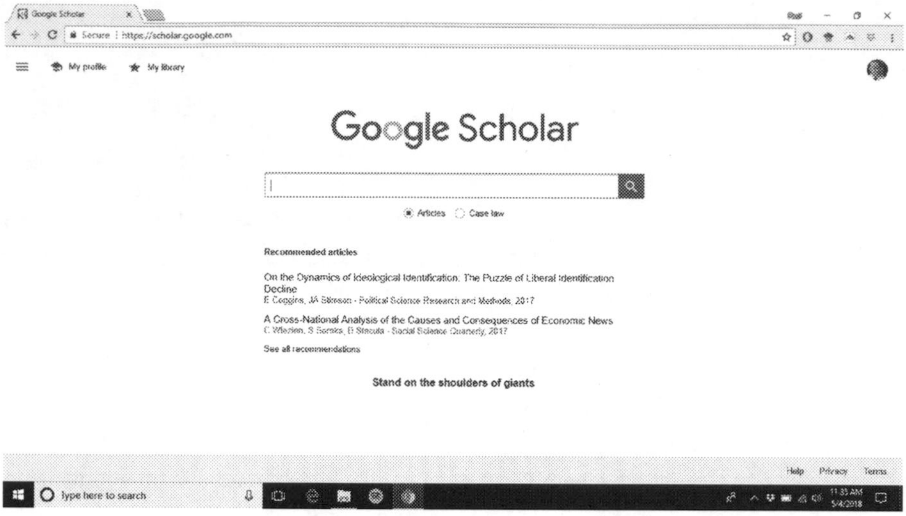

Figure 2.3 The Google Scholar home page

search for on the Internet, it has a dedicated search engine for scholarly publications like books and journal articles. The aspects of Google you're likely most familiar with come from Google's home page, www.google .com. The searches that they enable through scholarly work, however, using what they call "Google Scholar," is at a different site, https:// scholar.google.com. That site looks a good bit like Google's home page, but when you're at Google Scholar, it's searching a different corner of the Internet entirely – the part where academic journals and books are uploaded.

Figure 2.3 shows the Google Scholar home page. If you have a Google account (like a gmail address), you can save items in "My Library" – we'll show you how to do that shortly – that you can access any time. The articles are normally saved as an Adobe .PDF file. You'll notice the familiar search box that looks like Google's normal home page. You can tell from the figure, though, that, despite the similarities in appearances, this website is https://scholar.google.com.

So let's see how Google Scholar works. In the first chapter of *FSR*, we introduced you to what we called the theory of economic threat and attitudes toward immigrants. Let's see what happens when we type "economic threat and attitudes toward immigrants" in the Google Scholar search bar.

Figure 2.4 shows the results of that Google Scholar search. Let's examine that result. If you look to the far right of the fifth selection (the article by Bobo and Fox), you see the text "[PDF] jstor.org," which shows you what format the file is available in – in this case, an Adobe .PDF – and where – in this case, at the archive www.jstor.org. Your college or university's library almost surely has a subscription to JStor that your

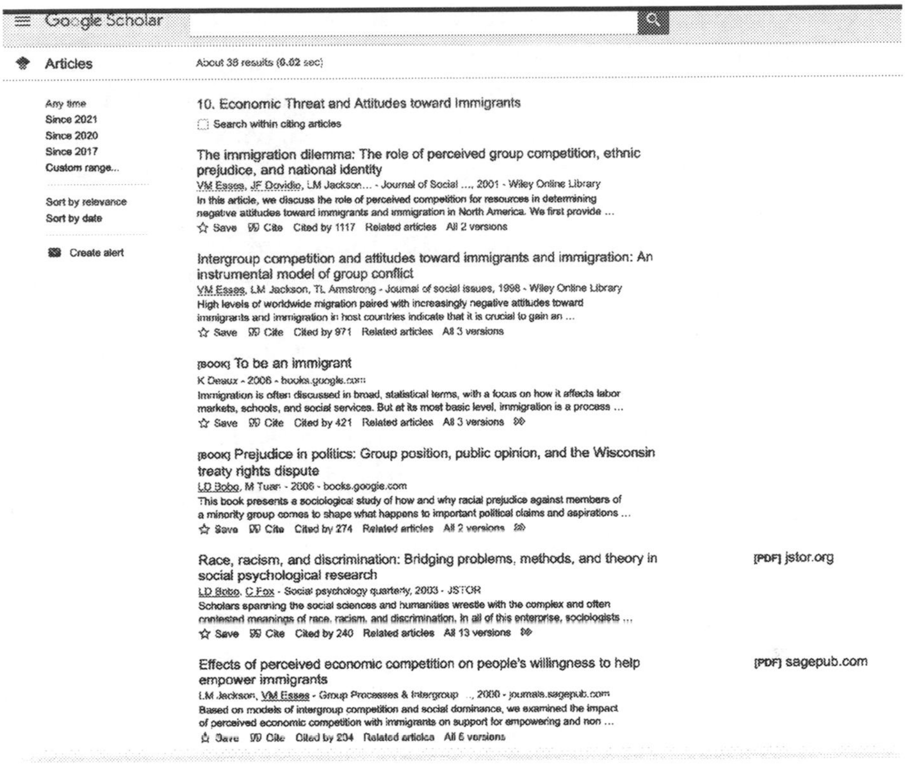

Figure 2.4 Google Scholar results for "economic threat and attitudes toward immigrants" search

student fees pay for, and so, if you're on a campus Internet connection (as opposed to a WiFi network at your home, or on a cellular network), clicking on "[PDF] jstor.org" will take you to the article. (If you're on your home WiFi network, then JStor doesn't know that you're a university student, and the publisher might ask you to pay a rather steep fee for access to the article. So beware about where you can do these searches for free.)

There's a lot of other information that the Google Scholar search reveals, though. First, if you want to save an entry to your "My Library," then click on the ☆ at the lower left of the item, and you'll be able to access that .PDF anywhere.

Importantly, you can also see how influential every article has been to date. In Figure 2.4, you can see text near the bottom of the first citation (the article by Esses et al.) that says "Cited by 1117" – which means that the article has been cited 1117 times to date.[4] That number indicates that the paper has been massively influential.[5]

---

[4] If you conduct that same search today, the number would surely be higher. Citations tend to accumulate over time.

[5] Of course, you should be careful to remember the original publication date when interpreting citation counts as a measure of impact. The Esses et al. article was published in 2001, so it's not as if some scholars who work in this area have somehow not yet heard

Of course, that doesn't necessarily mean that the 1117 other articles all cite the Esses et al. (2001) article approvingly. Some might; others might not. But being agreed with, or being "proved right," isn't the highest value in science. It's far better to be an influential part of an ongoing debate while being proved wrong in some respects, than it is to be indisputably correct but ignored by other scholars.

Perhaps you say to yourself, "Sure, Esses and her colleagues wrote an influential article on economic threat and attitudes toward immigrants a good long while ago. What kind of work is being done on the topic *now*?" This is one of the places where Google Scholar is fabulous. That "Cited by 1117" is clickable. You can literally see the list of all 1117 articles that cite the Esses article if you want. (Of course, it would take you a while to sift through them!) If you click on "Cited by 1117" and then choose "Since 2017" on the left side of the screen, you will see the number of citations that the Esses article has received since 2017. (You can pick "since" any year you like, obviously.) This is a good way to start the process of exploring a particular topic in academic writing that interests you.

Just like with using any Internet search engine, there's something of a skill in figuring out how to efficiently search for the material you want without getting bogged down with lots of results that aren't interesting to you. Should you use quotation marks in your search, or in a portion of your search terms? Sometimes yes, sometimes no. (In the example above, we did not.) As a general rule, it might be best to try it both ways to see if you get different results.

We have not exhausted all there is to know about how to use Google Scholar here, of course. For example, many scholars have created "Google Scholar profiles," which enables you to see the list of scholarly articles and books that they have authored, usually sorted from those with the most citations to the ones with the least. This can help you find similar articles, too, because many scholars work on a topic over the course of many years, and therefore their earlier articles are related to their more recent ones. In Figure 2.4, for example, you can see the scholars whose names are underlined; those are clickable links to those scholars' respective Google Scholar profiles. In addition, the "Help" section of Google Scholar is surprisingly helpful!

2.4 WRAPPING UP

In the main *FSR* text, we discussed how important it is that our theories be new and original – that is, that we aren't merely repeating the ideas and

---

of this article. But for an article published more recently – say in 2016 – its impact cannot yet fully be known. That merely means that we don't yet know if the article is likely to have a large impact. Only time will tell.

claims of previous scholars. One of the important preconditions for doing something genuinely new is to be familiar with the works that have already been produced on that same topic. Having the vast archive of journal articles and even many books available online – and freely accessible, thanks to your university's libraries – through storage sites like www .jstor.org has been the first step in making this task a lot easier than it was in decades past. The second step has been the invention of very sophisticated search engines like Google Scholar to help us find the previous studies that we otherwise might have missed.

2.5   EXERCISES

1. Conduct a search for the following terms using both Google's home page (www.google.com) and Google Scholar (https://scholar.google.com). Only include the quotation marks in your search if we include them. Report the similarities and differences you observe in the first page of the search results:

   (a) "economic threat and attitudes toward immigrants"

   (b) economic threat and attitudes toward immigrants

   (c) economic threat and prejudice

2. Open Stata and load the do-file named "Chapter 2 Bar Graph Example.do" into the do-file editor. Make sure that you have the correct directory path for loading the data. In other words, if "C:\MyFSRStataFiles" is not where you have your data, change this part of the do-file so that the data load into Stata.

   (a) Once you have done this, run the code to produce the graph presented in Figure 2.2 from *FSR*. Open a word processing document and then copy the figure from Stata and paste it into your word processing document.

   (b) Write a short summary of what you see in this figure.

3. Open Stata and load the do-file named "Chapter 2 Connected Graph Example.do" into the do-file editor. Make sure that you have the correct directory path for loading the data. In other words, if "C:\MyFSRStataFiles" is not where you have your data, change this part of the do-file so that the data load into Stata.

   (a) Once you have done this, run the code to produce the graph presented in Figure 2.1 from *FSR*. Open a word processing document and then copy the figure from Stata and paste it into your word processing document.

   (b) Write a short summary of what you see in this figure.

3 Evaluating Causal Relationships

3.1 OVERVIEW

Unlike the previous two chapters, in Chapters 3 through 6, there will not be any computer-based lessons in Stata. Not to worry, though. There will be more than enough time for intensive computer work later in the book. We promise!

In this abbreviated chapter, then, we offer some expanded exercises that will apply the lessons learned in the main text, and build on the skills from the first two chapters.

3.2 EXERCISES

1. Causal claims are common in media stories about news and politics. Sometimes they are explicitly stated, but often they are implicit. For each of the following news stories, identify the key causal claim in the story, and whether, based on the information given, you are convinced that all four causal hurdles have been crossed. (But remember that most media stories aren't the original generators of causal claims; they merely report on the news as they see fit to do so.)

   (a) www.cnn.com/2018/01/16/politics/freedom-house-democracy-trump-report/index.html

   (b) https://thehill.com/opinion/energy-environment/368355-wheres-the-proof-climate-change-causes-the-polar-vortex

   (c) www.foxnews.com/us/2018/01/16/california-mudslides-where-and-why-happen.html

   (d) www.aljazeera.com/news/2018/01/trump-muslim-ban-shifted-public-opinion-study-finds-180113092728118.html

   (e) www.npr.org/player/embed/575959966/576606076 (Podcast)

2. Candidates for public office make causal claims all the time. For each of the following snippets from a key speech made by a candidate, identify the key causal claim made in the speech, and whether, based on the information given, you are convinced that all four causal hurdles have been crossed. (But remember that candidates for office are not scientists responsible for testing causal claims; they are trying to persuade voters to support them over their opponent.)

   (a) "America is one of the highest-taxed nations in the world. Reducing taxes will cause new companies and new jobs to come roaring back into our country. Then we are going to deal with the issue of regulation, one of the greatest job-killers of them all. Excessive regulation is costing our country as much as $2 trillion a year, and we will end it. We are going to lift the restrictions on the production of American energy. This will produce more than $20 trillion in job creating economic activity over the next four decades." (Excerpt from Donald Trump's speech accepting the Republican nomination for President, July 21, 2016.)

   (b) "Now, I don't think President Obama and Vice President Biden get the credit they deserve for saving us from the worst economic crisis of our lifetimes. Our economy is so much stronger than when they took office. Nearly 15 million new private-sector jobs. Twenty million more Americans with health insurance. And an auto industry that just had its best year ever. That's real progress." (Excerpt from Hillary Clinton's speech accepting the Democratic nomination for President, July 28, 2016.)

   (c) "The truth is, on issue after issue that would make a difference in your lives – on health care and education and the economy – Sen. McCain has been anything but independent. He said that our economy has made 'great progress' under this president. He said that the fundamentals of the economy are strong. And when one of his chief advisers – the man who wrote his economic plan – was talking about the anxiety Americans are feeling, he said that we were just suffering from a 'mental recession,' and that we've become, and I quote, 'a nation of whiners.'" (Excerpt from Barack Obama's speech accepting the Democratic nomination for President, August 28, 2008.)

   (d) "His [Barack Obama's] policies have not helped create jobs, they have depressed them. And this I can tell you about where President Obama would take America: His plan to raise taxes on small business won't add jobs, it will eliminate them; ... And his trillion-dollar deficits will slow our economy, restrain employment, and cause wages to stall." (Excerpt from Mitt Romney's speech accepting the Republican nomination for President, August 30, 2012.)

3. Social science, as we have argued, revolves around the making and evaluation of causal claims. Find each of the following research articles – Google Scholar

makes it easy to do so – and then identify the key causal claim made in the article. Then produce a causal hurdles scorecard, and decide to what degree you are convinced that all four causal hurdles have been crossed. Some of the statistical material presented in the articles will, this early in the semester, be beyond your comprehension. That will change as the semester rolls along! (And remember that social scientists are trained to be experts in testing causal claims. So set the bar high.)

(a) Scarborough, W.J., Pepin, J.R., Lambouths III, D.L., Kwon, R., and Monasterio, R. 2021. "The intersection of racial and gender attitudes, 1977 through 2018." *American Sociological Review* 86(5):823–855.

(b) Perry, S.L., Cobb, R.J., Whitehead, A.L., and Grubbs, J.B. 2021. "Divided by faith (in Christian America): Christian nationalism, race, and divergent perceptions of racial injustice." *Social Forces*, soab134, https://doi.org/10.1093/sf/soab134.

(c) McLaren, L.M. 2003. "Anti-immigrant prejudice in Europe: Contact, threat perception, and preferences for the exclusion of migrants." *Social Forces* 81(3):909–936.

4 Research Design

4.1 OVERVIEW

As was the case in Chapter 3, there will not be any computer-based lessons in Stata. Again, we offer some expanded exercises that will apply the lessons learned in the main text.

4.2 EXERCISES

1. There are a lot of substantive problems in social science that we might *wish* to study experimentally, but which might seem to be impossible to study with experimental methods. (Recall from the main text (Section 4.2.3) that one of the drawbacks to conducting experiments is that not all X variables are subject to experimental control and random assignment.) Imagine the following causal questions, and write a paragraph about what would be required to conduct an experiment in that particular research situation, being careful to refer to both halves of the two-part definition of an experiment in your answer. (Warning: Some of them will seem impossible, or nearly impossible, or might require time travel.)

   (a) Does an individual's religiosity cause a person's level of opposition to same-sex marriage?

   (b) Does a country's openness to trade cause blue-collar workers' wages to fall?

   (c) Does having a more racially diverse set of school administrators and teachers cause a reduction in student suspensions and expulsions?

   (d) Does race cause differences between African American and white girls' experiences in the science classroom?

2. For each of the above research situations, if you were *unable* to perform an experiment, name at least one Z variable that could potentially confound the

$X-Y$ relationship, and would need to be controlled for in some other manner, in an observational study.

3. Assuming that you were unable to conduct an experiment for the aforementioned research situations, describe an observational study that you might conduct instead. In each case, is the study you envision a cross-sectional or time-series observational study? Why?

4. Consider the following research question: Does exposure to stories in the news media shape an individual's opinions on race- and/or gender-related policy issues (e.g., national policies on college admissions, hiring and promoting policies, etc.)?

    (a) Write a short paragraph trying to explain the causal mechanism that might be at work here.

    (b) If we wanted to study this relationship using an experiment, what would the barriers to conducting the experiment be?

    (c) What, if any, are the ethical considerations involved in studying that relationship experimentally?

    (d) What are the benefits of exploring that relationship experimentally? In other words, what specific Z variables would be controlled for in an experiment that could potentially be confounding in an observational study?

    (e) Read the following article and write a one-paragraph summary of it:

    King, G., Schneer, B., and White, A. 2017. "How the news media activate public expression and influence national agendas." *Science* 358:776–780.

5. Consider the relationship between the level of democracy in a country and the country's respect for human rights.

    (a) Describe both a cross-sectional and a time-series observational design that would help test the theory that increases in the level of democracy cause a country to increase its respect for human rights.

    (b) What concerns would you have about crossing the four causal hurdles in each case?

6. Write a one-paragraph summary of the following research articles:

    (a) Branton, R.P., and Jones, B.S. 2005. "Reexamining racial attitudes: The conditional relationship between diversity and socioeconomic environment." *American Journal of Political Science* 49(2):359–372.

    (b) Sullivan, J.M., and Ghara, A. 2015. "Racial identity and intergroup attitudes: A multiracial youth analysis." *Social Science Quarterly* 96(1):261–272.

(c) Bansak, K., Hainmueller, J., and Hangartner, D. 2016. "How economic, humanitarian, and religious concerns shape European attitudes toward asylum seekers." *Science* 354(6309):217–222.

In writing your summaries address the following questions:

  i. What was the research question/puzzle examined by the author(s)?

 ii. What was their theory?

iii. What was their research design?

 iv. How did they do with the four hurdles?

  v. What did they conclude?

5 Survey Research

OVERVIEW

As was the case in Chapters 3 and 4, there will not be any computer-based lessons in Stata. Again, we offer some expanded exercises that will apply the lessons learned in the main text.

5.2 EXERCISES

1. Select two articles from a social science journal that examine similar topics in an area of research interest to you, one that employs an experimental design and another that uses an observational design.

   (a) Provide a summary of each article, including a description of the dependent variable, the independent variable(s), and any Z variables. What is the primary causal mechanism, according to the authors, that links the independent and dependent variables? Which study do you think provides a more compelling answer to the research question?

   (b) Would it be feasible to combine the experimental and observational designs of the two studies that you selected in an effort to improve upon each?

2. In Exercise 5 in Chapter 5 of *FSR*, we asked you to describe a research question that you might be interested in examining using either the GSS or ANES data sets. We then asked you to describe how that research question might be expanded by using either the ISSP or WVS data sets. In this exercise, visit the website of either the GSS or ANES and the website of either the ISSP or WVS, depending on your selections in Chapter 5. Download to your computer the codebooks for the two data sets that you chose, and identify the variables that you would use to measure your key concepts.

6 Measuring Concepts of Interest

6.1 OVERVIEW

As was the case in Chapters 3, 4, and 5, there will not be any computer-based lessons in Stata. Again, we offer some expanded exercises that will apply the lessons learned in the main text.

6.2 EXERCISES

1. Consider, for a moment, the concept of "customer satisfaction." For now, let's define it as "the degree to which a product or service meets or exceeds a customer's expectations." So, like other concepts, it is a variable: Some customers are very satisfied, some have mixed experiences, and some are very unhappy. Companies – and even some government agencies – are interested for obvious reasons in understanding that variation. Now answer the following questions:

   (a) How well do you think Yelp reviews serve as a measure of customer satisfaction? Explain your answer.

   (b) Read "The Happiness Button" in the February 5, 2018 issue of *The New Yorker*: www.newyorker.com/magazine/2018/02/05/customer-satisfaction-at-the-push-of-a-button. What are the strengths and weaknesses of the strategy pursued by HappyOrNot in terms of measuring the concept of customer satisfaction?

   (c) The article describes the push-button measures of satisfaction at security checkpoints in London's Heathrow Airport. What are the strengths and weaknesses of such an approach? If, on a particular day, there was a higher share of "frown" responses, what would that tell (and what wouldn't that tell) to the officials at Heathrow?

2. The concept of "religiosity" is a very important one in sociology, as it lies at the heart of many influential theories of why citizens hold the opinions that

they do, including views of racial/ethnic minorities and homosexuality, and why they vote the way that they do. Answer the following questions:

(a) Conceptually, how would you define religiosity? Try to be as specific as possible.

(b) Measuring religiosity, as you might imagine, can be a bit tricky. The flagship specialty journal in the area of the sociology of religion is the *Journal for the Scientific Study of Religion* (hereafter *JSSR*). Go to the website for *JSSR* and search for articles that include "religiosity" in their titles. Read several of them, beginning with the most recent ones and working your way back to earlier issues of the journal. Make a list of the various questions that the authors use in their operational definitions of religiosity and the rationales that they use for doing so. Can you think of an alternative measurement strategy for this concept?

3. The concept of "consumer confidence" is important in the study of economics and political science, among other disciplines.

(a) Go to https://news.google.com and search for "consumer confidence" (and be sure to use the quotation marks). From the search results, pick a recent news article that discusses consumer confidence. (Print out the article and include it with your homework.) How well, if at all, does the article define consumer confidence, or how it is measured?

(b) From what you know, offer a conceptual definition of consumer confidence.

(c) There are two major surveys in the U.S. that measure consumer confidence on monthly intervals. One of them is the Survey of Consumers at the University of Michigan. They produce what they call an Index of Consumer Sentiment, which is composed of responses to five survey items. One of the five is as follows:

> Looking ahead, which would you say is more likely – that in the country as a whole we'll have continuous good times during the next five years or so, or that we will have periods of widespread unemployment or depression, or what?

What are the potential strengths and weaknesses of this survey question as one component of consumer confidence?

(d) All five of the items in the Michigan Index of Consumer Sentiment can be found here: https://data.sca.isr.umich.edu/fetchdoc.php?docid=24770. How are the five items similar to one another, and how are they different from one another?

(e) The complete monthly survey can be found here: https://data.sca.isr.umich
.edu/fetchdoc.php?docid=24776. You will note that the survey does not
contain *any* questions to measure a survey respondent's political beliefs or
affiliations. Why do you think that is the case?

(f) Can you think of any additional survey questions that might complement
or replace the ones in the Michigan Index?

7 Getting to Know Your Data

7.1 OVERVIEW

In this chapter we introduce you to the commands needed to produce descriptive statistics and graphs using Stata. If you're feeling a little rusty on the basics of Stata that we covered in Chapters 1 and 2, it would be good to review them before diving into this chapter.

In Chapter 7 of *FSR* we discussed a variety of tools that can be used to get to know your data one variable at a time. In this chapter, we discuss how to produce output in Stata to allow you to get to know your variables. An important first step to getting to know your data is to figure out what is the measurement metric for each variable. For categorical and ordinal variables, we suggest producing frequency tables. For continuous variables, there are a wide range of descriptive statistics and graphs.

7.2 DESCRIBING CATEGORICAL AND ORDINAL VARIABLES

As we discussed in Chapter 7 of *FSR*, a frequency table is often the best way to numerically examine and present the distribution of values for a categorical or ordinal variable. In Stata, the "tabulate" command is used to produce frequency tables. In a do-file or from the command line, the syntax for this command is

```
tabulate variable
```

where `variable` is the name of the variable for which you want the frequencies. This command produces a four-column table in which the first column contains the variable values (or value labels if there are value labels for this variable), the second column is the number of cases in the data set that take on each value, the third column is the percentage of cases that take on each value, and the fourth column is the cumulative percentage of cases from top to bottom.

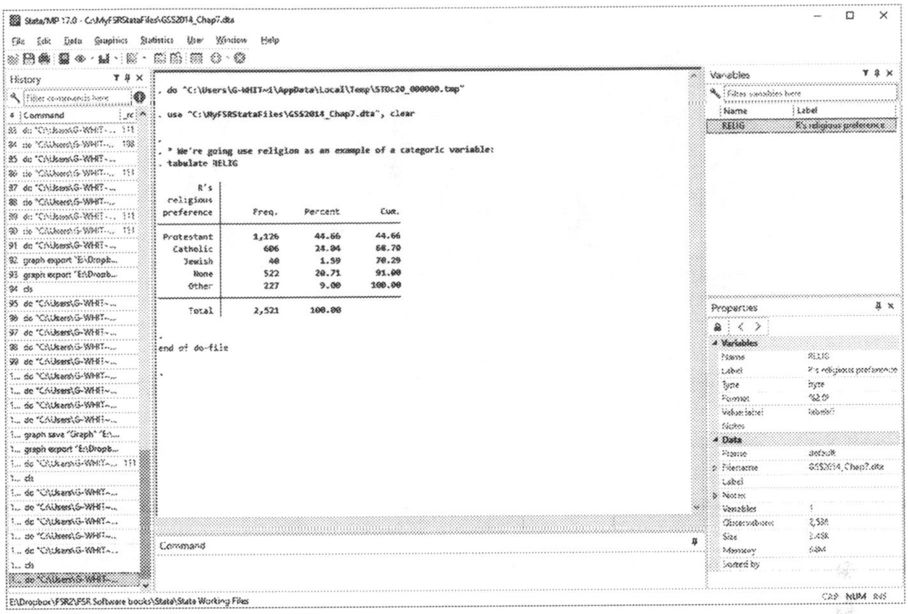

Figure 7.1 Raw output from tabulate command

The data presented in Table 7.1 of *FSR* are an example of the output obtained from using the "tabulate" command. These results were generated using the data set GSS2014_sample_chap7.dta which can be found in the Stata directory at www.cambridge.org/fsr. The output from this use of the "tabulate" command is displayed in Figure 7.1. Take a moment to compare the table in Figure 7.1 here with Table 7.1 of *FSR*. Although both tables convey the same information, Table 7.1 of *FSR* does so in a more polished fashion. This is an example of why we don't want to copy from the Stata output and paste that into our papers or presentations. Instead, it is important to craft tables so that they convey what is most necessary and don't include a lot of extra information. We'll have more to say about making tables in Chapter 8 (and forward) in this workbook.

Pie graphs, such as Figure 7.1 in *FSR*, are a graphical way to get to know categorical and ordinal variables.[1] The syntax to produce a pie graph in a do-file or from the command line is

```
graph pie, over(variable)
```

As an example of this, we can create a pie graph like that in Figure 7.1 of *FSR* with the following line of code:

```
graph pie, over(RELIG) scheme(s1mono)
```

which will produce a pie graph like the one displayed in Figure 7.2.

---

[1] Once you've created a graph in Stata, which opens as a new window, you can click on that graph and use Stata's Graph Editor to customize the axis labels, colors, and the like. Try it!

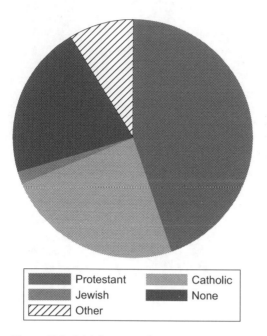

Figure 7.2 Initial pie graph

As we discuss is Chapter 7 of *FSR*, statisticians strongly prefer bar graphs to pie charts because bar graphs, especially when they have been sorted by the frequency with which the value occurs, make it easier for one to make assessments about the relative frequency of different values. The easiest way to obtain a figure like this in Stata is to run the following two commands:

```
generate variable1=variable2

graph bar (count) variable1, over(variable2, sort((count)
variable1) descending)
```

where `variable1` is the name of the variable for which you want the frequencies displayed in a bar graph, and `variable2` is the same variable duplicated.

As an example of this, we can create a bar graph like that in Figure 7.1 of *FSR* with the following lines of code:

```
gen RELIGa=RELIG
graph bar (count) RELIG, /*
*/ over(RELIGa, sort((count) RELIG) descending)
scheme(s1mono)
```

This would produce the bar graph displayed in Figure 7.3. Note, though, that Figure 7.3 is not exactly like Figure 7.2 of *FSR*. To produce something closer to this figure in appearance, we need the following command:

```
graph bar (count) RELIG, /*
*/ ytitle("Number of Cases") scheme(s1mono) /*
*/ over(RELIGa, sort((count) RELIG) descending /*
*/ relabel(1 "Protestant" 2 "Catholic" 3 "None" 4 "Jewish"
5 "Other"))
```

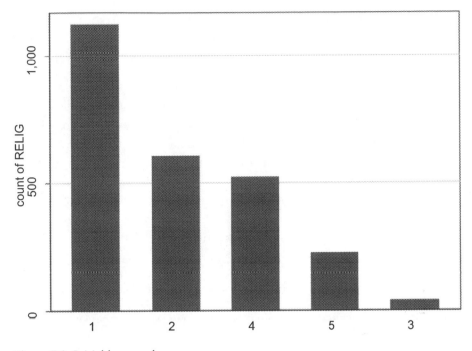

Figure 7.3 Initial bar graph

where, as we have seen before, "ytitle" tells Stata that we want to make our own label for the vertical axis, and "relabel" tells Stata that we want to provide text labels for each of the bars instead of the numbers that it places by default along the horizontal axis of the figure.

7.3 DESCRIBING CONTINUOUS VARIABLES

While the values for categorical variables in a sample of data can easily be presented in a frequency table, this is usually not the case for continuous variables. Consider Table 7.2 in *FSR*. To produce this table, we ran the following two commands for the variable "Pct_Own_Home":

```
sort Pct_Own_Home
list year Pct_Own_Home
```

where "sort" tells Stata to sort the observations in our data set from the smallest value to the largest value of a particular variable and "list" tells Stata that we want to see, in the output window, the values of a particular variable or set of variables whose names we provide. Even for a relatively small data set, such as that presented in Table 7.2 in *FSR*, this output provides a lot of information. For this reason, we turn to summary statistics when we want to describe continuous variables. To use a metaphor, with summary statistics, we are looking at the broad contours of the forest rather than examining each individual tree.

Figure 7.2 in *FSR* displays the output from Stata's "summarize" command with the "detail" option. As we discuss in *FSR*, this command produces a full battery of descriptive statistics for a continuous variable. The syntax for this command is

```
summarize variable, detail
```

where the "detail" option tells Stata that we want a full set of output summarizing the values of a particular variable. From the discussion in Chapter 7, we can see that Stata's "summarize" command with the "detail" option presents both rank statistics and moment statistics to describe the values taken on by continuous variables.

This command can also be used to produce summaries of the values for more than one variable by writing

```
summarize variable1 variable2, detail
```

or, if we want this information for all variables in a data set, we would modify the command by simply leaving out the names of any variables and writing

```
summarize , detail
```

Though, if we want summaries of many or all of the variables in a data set, we recommend leaving off the "detail" option and writing simply

```
summarize
```

An example of the output that this produces is displayed in Figure 7.4.

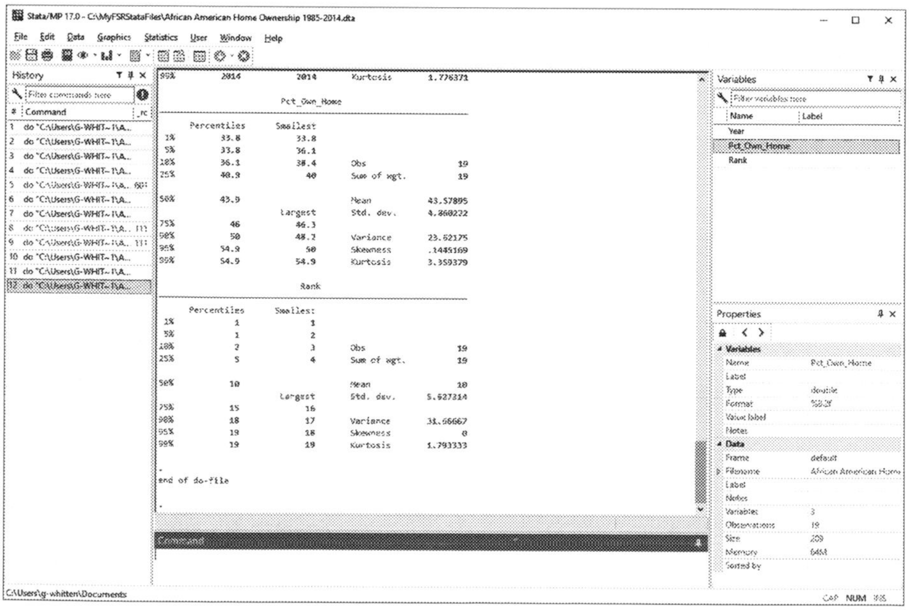

Figure 7.4 Results from running a summarize, detail command

While statistical summaries of variables are helpful, it is also sometimes quite helpful to also look at visual summaries of the values for a variable. To get a visual depiction of rank statistics, we recommend producing a box–whisker plot like that displayed in Figure 7.3 in *FSR*. The syntax for a box–whisker plot of the values for a single continuous variable is

```
graph box variable
```

To get a visual depiction of moment statistics, we recommend producing either a histogram, such as in Figures 7.5 and 7.6 from *FSR*, or a kernel density plot, such as in Figure 7.7 from *FSR*. The syntax for a histogram of the values for a single continuous variable is

```
histogram variable
```

From a do-file or from the command line, the syntax for a kernel density plot of the values for a single continuous variable is

```
kdensity variable
```

In order to produce a histogram and kernel density plot combined in one figure, like in Figure 7.8 of *FSR*, we can take advantage of the fact that both `histogram` and `kdensity` commands are specific members of Stata's comprehensive `twoway` graphics command. We can produce a single figure that combines a histogram and a kernel density plot for the same variable (in this case, Pct_Own_Home) with

```
twoway histogram Pct_Own_Home || kdensity Pct_Own_Home,
scheme(s1mono)
```

in which `twoway histogram` tells Stata that we want to produce a graph from the "twoway" set of graphs and that the specific type of twoway graph that we want is a histogram, and the "||" is a way of telling Stata that we want the resulting figure to contain another twoway figure. Note that we do not need to repeat "`twoway`" in front of "`kdensity`" in this command.

The resulting output is displayed in Figure 7.5. Although this figure looks pretty good, we don't particularly like the legend underneath. Since both a histogram and a kernel density plot are ways of showing the density of the values for a variable, we can get rid of this legend and label the vertical axis in this figure as Density. This can be done with the following command:

```
twoway histogram Pct_Own_Home /*
*/ || kdensity Pct_Own_Home /*
*/ , scheme(s1mono) legend(off) ytitle("Density") /*
*/ xtitle(" " "African American Home Ownership Percentage")
```

where `legend(off)` tells Stata that we do not want the legend and `ytitle("Density")` tells Stata how to label the vertical axis.

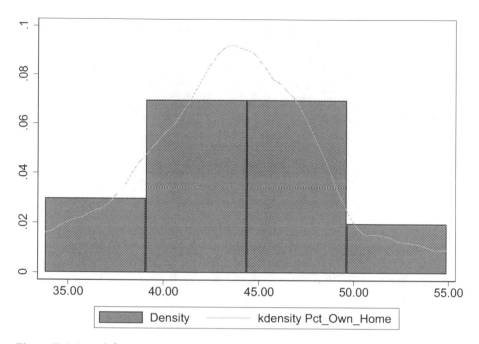

Figure 7.5 Initial figure combining a histogram and kernel density plot for incumbent vote

7.4 PUTTING STATISTICAL OUTPUT INTO TABLES, DOCUMENTS, AND PRESENTATIONS

So you've generated some statistical output for the first time. Congratulations! But now what do you do? As you can tell from the descriptions above, we think it's important to be thoughtful about how to present your results to your audience. That's why we went to great lengths to show you commands to make the graphics appear in the most interpretable way possible. The same is true with data that you wish to include in a tabular format. We emphasize that just copying and pasting output from Stata (or any other program) is unlikely to impress your audience – even if your audience is "just" your professor or teaching assistant.

For example, when we produce descriptive statistics in Stata using either the "tabulate" or "summarize" commands, we get a *lot* of output. Usually this output is much more than what we need to present in a paper that describes our variables one at a time. We therefore suggest making your own tables in whatever word processing program you are working with.

Graphs are a bit simpler, though. Once you have a graph that meets the standards we've outlined above, and you want to include in a document, one of the easiest ways to do so is to right-click on the graph in Stata and select "copy" and then right-click on the location where you want to place the graph in your word processing program and select "paste." Depending on the word processor, you might just want to resize the graphic image by clicking on the corner of the image and dragging the image to be bigger or smaller, depending on what would look best in your paper or presentation.

We'll have more to say about this topic in Chapter 8, and forward, as we introduce new statistical techniques to you. The upshot, though, is always the same: Put some care into what you present to your audience. The amount of attention you devote to the details – low or high – will be obvious to your audience.

7.5 EXERCISES

1. Open Stata and load the do-file named "Chapter 7 Categorical Variable Example.do" into the do-file editor. Make sure that you have the correct directory path for loading the data. In other words, if "C:\MyFSRStataFiles" is not where you have your data, change this part of the do-file so that the data load into Stata.

   Once you have done this, run the code to produce the graphs like those presented in Figures 7.1 and 7.2 from *FSR*. Open a word processing document and then copy these figures from Stata and paste them into your word processing document.

2. Open Stata and load the do-file named "Chapter 7 Continuous Variable Example.do" into the do-file editor. Make sure that you have the correct directory path for loading the data. In other words, if "C:\MyFSRStataFiles" is not where you have your data, change this part of the do-file so that the data load into Stata.

   Once you have done this, run the code to create a box–whisker plot, a histogram, a kernel density plot, and a combined histogram and kernel density plot. Copy and paste each of these figures into your word processing document.

8 Probability and Statistical Inference

8.1 OVERVIEW

In this chapter, we teach you how to use a computer simulation using a preprogrammed Excel spreadsheet. The goal of this chapter is to familiarize you with some of the basics of how probability works, and especially to see how sample sizes come into play.

8.2 DICE ROLLING IN EXCEL

There are a variety of free spreadsheets available online that simulate the rolling of dice.[1] The one we will use is available at the Stata link at www.cambridge.org/fsr.

Right-click on the filename "diceroller.xls" and save it to your computer.[2] Find the file and open it. What you'll see should look like Figure 8.1.

The spreadsheet is quite simple: It contains a basic program that simulates the rolling of two six-sided dice, with a graphic display of the resulting dice faces, as well as output data to keep track of the rolls. The sheet basically contains three sections. In the top left of the sheet are the two dice. In the launch screen in Figure 8.1, those dice are a 5 and a 1. There are also buttons there to roll the dice – you can click the "Roll 'em (Ctrl+R)" button or press "Ctrl" and "R" on your keyboard. You can click the "Clear History" button to erase the history of rolls and start over.

The history of rolls of the two dice are displayed along the lower-left side of the sheet. In that section, there are columns of data that correspond to the roll number ("Roll #"), the roll of die 1 ("D1"), the roll of die 2 ("D2"), and the sum of die 1 and die 2 ("Tot"). In Figure 8.1, since we

---

[1] Google "spreadsheet dice roller" to find several of them.

[2] Unfortunately, the functionality of the spreadsheet only works in Microsoft Excel, so if you're used to using Google Sheets, you'll need to be on a computer that has Microsoft Excel installed on it.

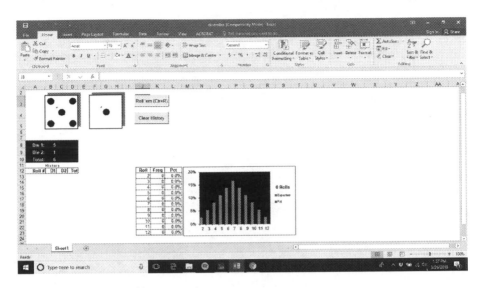

Figure 8.1 The dice roller in Excel

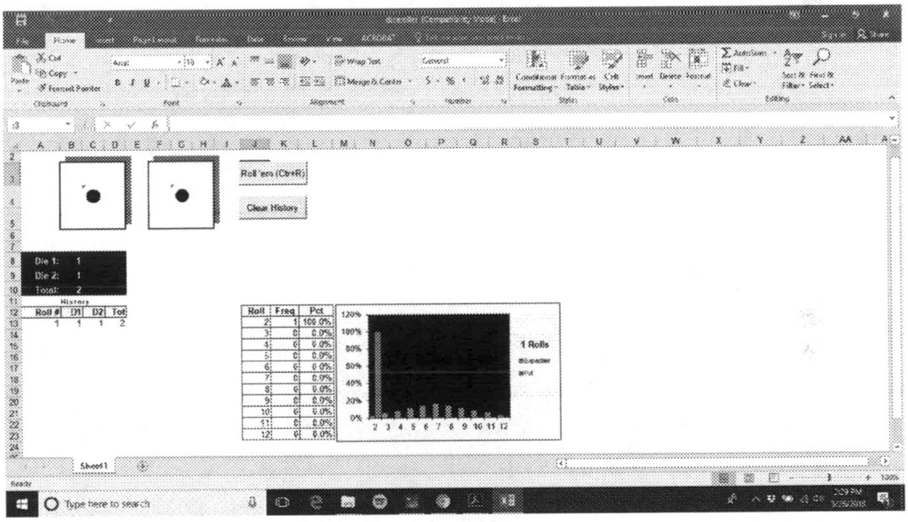

Figure 8.2 The results of our first roll

haven't rolled the dice yet, you will see that in the rows beneath the display of "Roll #, D1, D2, Tot," the cells are all empty. When we begin rolling the dice, those rows will begin to fill up.

The third section of the sheet, in the lower right, shows the actual sum of the two dice (from the "Tot" column) – which will appear in red bars – as well as the distribution that we would *expect* to see given that the dice are fair – shown in gray bars.

Let's go ahead and roll the dice, either by hovering your mouse over the "Roll 'em" button and left-clicking it or hitting "Ctrl" and "R" on

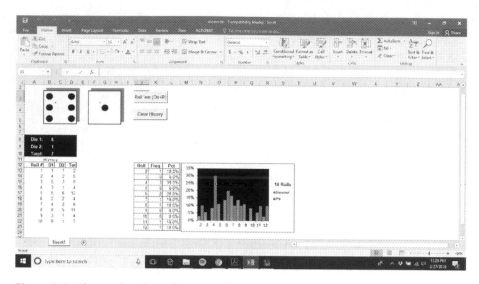

Figure 8.3 The results of our first ten rolls

your keyboard. The results of our first roll are in Figure 8.2. As you can see, we rolled a "snake eyes" – a 1 and a 1. (Obviously, when you're doing this on your own computer, you might roll something different!) All of the output looks as you'd expect. In the lower left of the sheet, you see that, for roll 1, die 1 was a 1 and die 2 was also a 1, making the total (the sum) 2 (because 1 plus 1 equals 2). That's reflected in the graph on the lower-right portion of the sheet, with a large red bar at the spot for 2, indicating that all 100 percent of rolls so far totalled a 2.

Let's click "Roll 'em" a few more times, so that we get ten rolls in total.

Figure 8.3 shows the results of the first ten rolls that we performed when writing this chapter. (Again, the outcomes of your rolls are quite likely to be different than ours!) You'll notice from the figure that we haven't rolled another "snake eyes." In fact, we've rolled three 4s, two 6s, and the other five results just one apiece.

We can roll the dice as many times as we'd like. (Just press "Ctrl" and "R" on your keyboard repeatedly. Yes, that means pressing it 100 times if you want 100 rolls, or 1000 times if you want 1000 rolls.) Go ahead and roll the dice around 100 times, and watch the red and gray bars shift as you do. (For our purposes right now, it doesn't matter if you roll them exactly 100 times.)

Figure 8.4 shows our results. As always, your rolls will be different from the ones we got. Let's examine the results in the figure. As you can see from the output screen and associated bar graph, we have rolled a total of 4 – either through a 1 and a 3, or a pair of 2s, or a 3 and a 1 – fifteen

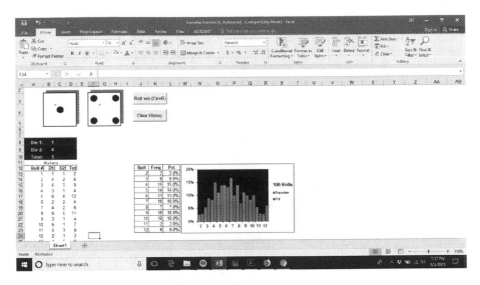

Figure 8.4 The results of our first 100 rolls

times out of 100. That's more than would be expected by chance. You can also see that we've managed to roll double 6s six times out of the 100 rolls again, more than would be expected. Perhaps the biggest discrepancy between the observed outcomes in red and the expected ones in gray is in the rolls that total 8. For whatever reason, we rolled about half as many 8s as would have been expected by chance.

Let's be clear: None of the above is meant to imply a judgment – positive or negative – on what we've found. In theory, there are a "squadpillion" possible rolls of these two dice, and what we've just done is sample one, then ten, and then 100 of them. At the extreme, rolling the two dice just one time produced a rather odd – by definition! – "outcome." Every single roll (of that one roll!) was a 2! How weird is that? Of course, for a single roll, *any* outcome would have been "odd" in this sense. As we move from one roll to ten to 100, though, we start to see the beginning of convergence between what we observe and what we expect to observe. Will the observed outcomes ever *exactly* equal the expected ones? Probably not.

One other thing that Excel allows us to do is to calculate the averages of the rolls of the individual die, and of the dice collectively. Doing so is straightforward. For example, if we want to calculate the average of the rolls of die 1, we can go anywhere in the spreadsheet and type

```
=average(b13:b112)
```

and hit the "Enter" key on your keyboard. (You'll see that we performed this in cell b114, because it is below the bottom of the string of cells for which we are calculating the mean, with a single space in between the last

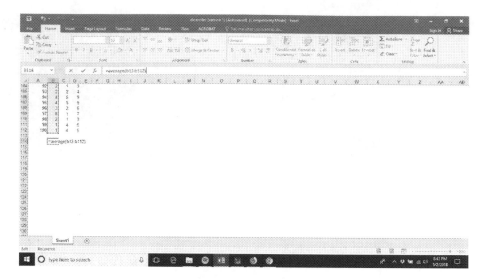

Figure 8.5 How to calculate the average of our first 100 rolls of die 1

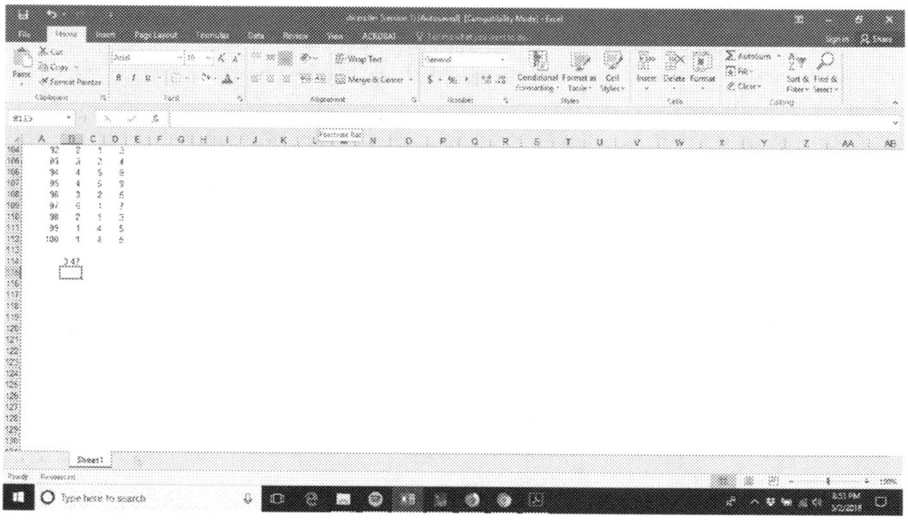

Figure 8.6 The result of calculating the average of our first 100 rolls of die 1

cell of data – cell b112 – and where we want our mean to be displayed.) That process is displayed in Figure 8.5, before we hit the "Enter" key. When we hit the "Enter" key, of course, the result will appear.

As you can see in Figure 8.6, the average of our 100 rolls of die 1 is 3.47. (We repeat the admonition that, when you perform this in your own spreadsheet, you will almost certainly get different results.) When we repeat the process – that is, type

```
=average(c13:c112)
```

in cell c114 – for die 2, we find a different result, as is evident in Figure 8.7.

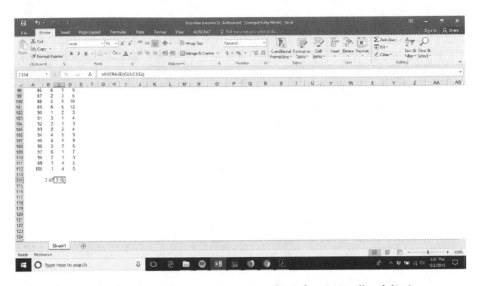

Figure 8.7 The result of calculating the average of our first 100 rolls of die 2

Figure 8.8 The result of calculating the average of our first 100 rolls of the sum of dice 1 and 2

That mean is 3.15. Does that figure seem "too low" to you? (And why did we type "too low" in scare quotes just there?) Obviously, in a mathematical sense, the result of 3.15 for die 2 is lower than the outcome of 3.47 for die 1: 3.15 < 3.47, we all know. We have computed the average of the sum of dice 1 and 2 in column D.

That result is displayed in Figure 8.8, and shows that the mean is 6.62. Because the mean of the rolls of die 1 is 3.47, and the mean of the rolls of die 2 is 3.15, the fact that the mean of the sum is 6.62 should not be surprising (3.47 + 3.15 = 6.62).

8.3 **EXERCISES**

1. In Figure 8.1 from the dice rolling module in Excel, before we actually roll any dice, what should we *expect* the mean of a set of rolls of a single die to be? Why? And what should we expect the mean of the sum of the rolls of two dice to be? Why? How do these numbers compare to the outcomes we found in Figures 8.6, 8.7, and 8.8?

2. In Figure 8.2, you notice that we happened to roll two 1s. Given that, what is the probability of rolling two 1s on the next roll? Explain your answer.

3. You've surely noticed that the gray bars in the dice rolling module in Excel – representing the "expected" rolls – in all of the dice figures seem to be shaped almost like a normal distribution. Why is that? Be careful in answering this question, and try to be as explicit as possible in arriving at your answer.

4. If you haven't already, in the dice rolling module in Excel, roll your dice 100 times. What are the means of die 1, die 2, and the sum of the two? How do these numbers compare to the outcomes we found in Figures 8.6, 8.7, and 8.8? What do you make of these similarities or differences?

5. Using the dice rolling module in Excel, roll the dice until the "observed" bars (in red) *roughly* approximate the gray "expected" bars. How many rolls did it take? Print out (or take a screenshot) of your output and turn it in with your answer.

9 Bivariate Hypothesis Testing

OVERVIEW

We are now ready to start testing hypotheses! As we discuss in Chapter 9 of *FSR*, bivariate hypothesis tests, or hypothesis tests carried out with only two variables, are seldom used as the primary means of hypothesis testing in social science research today. But it is imperative to understand the basic mechanics of bivariate hypothesis tests before moving to more complicated tests. This same logic applies to the use of statistical computing software. In this chapter, we teach you how to conduct hypothesis tests using the four techniques presented in Chapter 9 of *FSR*: tabular analysis, difference of means, the correlation coefficient, and analysis of variance.

9.2 **TABULAR ANALYSIS**

In tabular analysis, we are testing the null hypothesis that the column variable and row variable are unrelated to each other. We will review the basics of producing a table in which the rows and columns are defined by the values of two different variables, generating hypothesis-testing statistics, and then presenting what you have found.

The Stata syntax for producing a two-variable table is

```
tab2 rowvariable colvariable, column
```

where "*rowvariable*" is usually the dependent variable (with its values displayed across rows in the table) and "*colvariable*" is usually the independent variable (with its values displayed down the columns in the table). The option "column" tells Stata that, in addition to the frequency of values (or number of cases) being displayed in each cell, this command should produce column percentages for each row beneath the frequencies. As detailed in Chapter 9 of *FSR*, these column percentages allow for

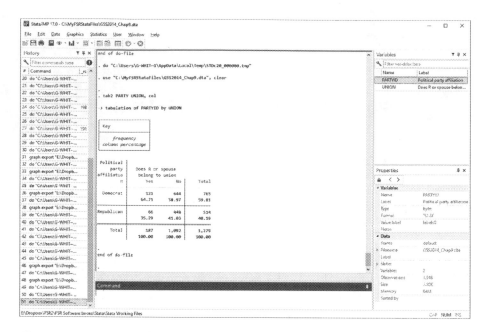

Figure 9.1 Raw output from tab2 command

the comparison of interest – they tell us how the dependent variable values differ in terms of their distribution across values of the independent variable.

It is crucial, when working with tables of this nature, to put the appropriate variables across the rows and columns of the table and then to present the column frequencies. For example, to recreate Table 9.2 in *FSR* we first run the command

```
tab2 PARTY UNION, col
```

where "PARTY" is a categorical variable that takes on a value of "1" if the respondent reported being a Democrat and "2" if the respondent reported being a Republican, and "UNION" is a variable that takes on a value of "1" if the respondent reported that they or their spouse belonged to a union and "2" otherwise.

The output from this running command is displayed in Figure 9.1. Take a moment to compare this raw output with Table 9.2 in *FSR*. There are two notable differences. First, in order to isolate the numbers needed for the assessment at hand (whether or not respondents from union households were affiliated with political parties differently from respondents from nonunion households), we need only the column percentages. And, second, we have added a note making it clear what are the values reported in each cell of the table.

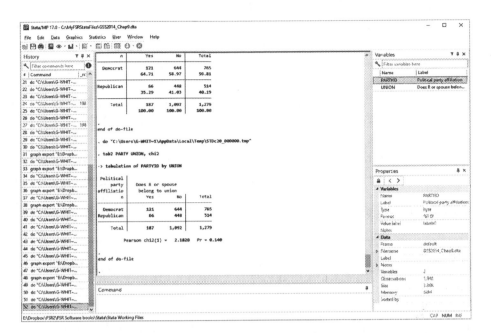

Figure 9.2 Raw output from tab2 command with the chi2 option

9.2.1 Generating Test Statistics

In Chapter 9 of *FSR* we discuss in detail the logic of Pearson's chi-squared test statistic, which we use to test the null hypothesis that the row and column variables are not related. To get this test statistic and the associated *p*-value for a two-variable table in Stata from a do-file or from the command line, the syntax for producing a two-variable table is

```
tab2 rowvariable colvariable, chi2
```

where, again, "`rowvariable`" is usually the dependent variable (with its values displayed across rows in the table) and "`colvariable`" is usually the independent variable (with its values displayed down the columns in the table). The option "chi2" tells Stata to report a chi-squared test statistic and the associated *p*-value. Thus, to conduct the chi-squared test for these variables like that in Section 9.4.1 of *FSR*, we would issue the command

```
tab2 PARTY UNION, chi2
```

which produces the output displayed in Figure 9.2.

9.2.2 Putting Tabular Results into Papers

We recommend that you make your own tables in whatever word processing program you choose to use instead of copying and pasting the tables that you make in Stata. The first reason for doing so is that you will think about your results more closely when you are producing your own tables. This will help you to catch any mistakes that you might have made and to write more effectively about what you have found. Another reason for doing so is that tables constructed by you will tend to look better. By controlling how the tables are constructed, you will be able to communicate with maximum clarity.

As a part of making your own tables, you should have the goal in mind that your table communicates something on its own. In other words, if someone *only* looked at your table, would they be able to figure out what was going on? If the answer is "yes," then you have constructed an effective table. We offer the following advice ideas for making useful tables:

- Give your tables a title that conveys the essential result in your table.
- Make your column and row headings as clear as possible.
- Put notes at the bottom of your tables to explain the table's contents.

9.3 DIFFERENCE OF MEANS

Difference of means tests are conducted when we have a continuous dependent variable and a limited independent variable.

9.3.1 Examining Differences Graphically

When we use graphs to assess a difference of means, we are graphing the distribution of the continuous dependent variable for two or more values of the limited independent variable. Figures 9.1 and 9.2 of *FSR* show how this is done with a box–whisker plot. The syntax for producing two box–whisker plots side-by-side is

```
graph box depvariable, over(indvariable)
```

where "`depvariable`" is the name of the continuous dependent variable and "`indvariable`" is the name of the limited independent variable. The code for producing a figure like Figures 9.1 and 9.2 of *FSR* combined is[1]

```
graph box EDUC, /*
*/ over(raceeth1, relabel(1 "Non-Hispanic White
2 "Non-Hispanic Black")) /*
*/ ytitle("Highest year of school completed" " ")
scheme(s1mono)
```

where the variable "EDUC" is the highest year of school completion and "raceeth1" is a categorical variable equal to 1 if the respondent identified as a non-Hispanic white and 2 if the respondent identified as a non-Hispanic black.

---

[1] The "/*" and "*/" in the commands indicate a multi-line command.

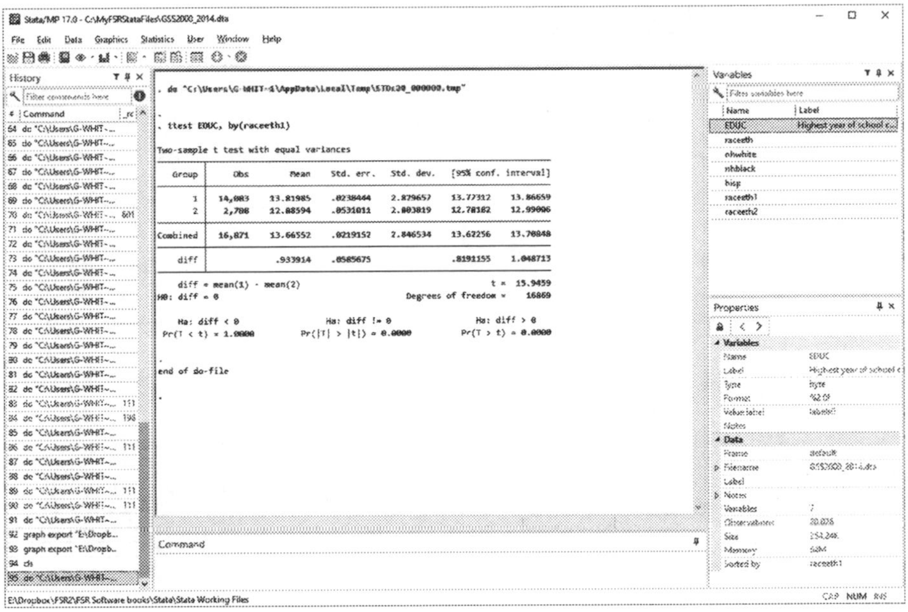

Figure 9.3 Raw output from ttest command

9.3.2 Generating Test Statistics

To conduct a difference of means *t*-test such as the one discussed in Chapter 9 of *FSR*, the syntax is:

```
ttest depvariable, by(indvariable)
```

For the *t*-test that we present in Chapter 9 of *FSR*, the syntax is

```
ttest EDUC, by(raceeth1)
```

which produces the output displayed in Figure 9.3 here. From this figure, we can see that the output from a difference of means *t*-test like this produces a lot of output. The first part of this output is a table of descriptive statistics for the dependent variable across each value of the independent variable and then overall. Much of this information is like that presented in Table 9.9 of *FSR*. We then get the *t*-statistic for this test (15.9459) and the *p*-value for the associated hypothesis test (0.0000 through four decimal digits).[2]

---

[2] You will notice that there are three hypothesis tests presented at the bottom of Figure 9.3. The one that we present in *FSR* is the middle one, which is expressed as "Ha: diff != 0". In Chapter 10 of *FSR* we get deeper into the business of different types of hypotheses and, more specifically, the difference between a hypothesis test like the one that we conducted and hypothesis tests like the others listed in Figure 9.3.

9.4   CORRELATION COEFFICIENTS

Correlation coefficients summarize the relationship between two continuous variables. They are also an important building block to understanding the basic mechanics of two-variable regression models.

9.4.1   Producing Scatter Plots

We can examine the relationship between two continuous variables in a scatter plot such as Figure 9.3 in *FSR*. The syntax for producing such a figure is

```
twoway scatter depvariable indvariable
```

If we run this code for our running example of support for government assistance as the dependent variable and the unemployment rate as the independent variable,

```
twoway scatter GovtAsst Unempl, scheme(s1mono)
```

we get the graph displayed in Figure 9.4 here. The code for producing a figure like Figure 9.3 in *FSR* is

```
twoway scatter GovtAsst Unempl, /*
*/ ytitle("Percentage Support for Government Assistance to
the Poor" " ") /*
*/ xtitle(" " "Unemployment Rate") /*
*/ msymbol(Oh) /*
*/ scheme(s1mono)
```

where "msymbol(Oh)" tells Stata to make large hollow circles instead of the default filled-in circles that we see in Figure 9.4. These open symbols make it a little bit easier to see overlapping data points.

9.4.2   Generating Covariance Tables and Test Statistics

To generate the output for a covariance table like Table 9.11 in *FSR*, the syntax is

```
correlate variable1 variable2, covariance
```

As you can probably guess, "correlate" is a command that can be used to produce correlation coefficients and the option "covariance" produces a covariance table. Continuing with the same running example, we can produce the output needed to create Table 9.11 in *FSR* by running

```
correlate GovtAsst Unempl, covariance
```

The following command

```
pwcorr depvariable indvariable, cov
```

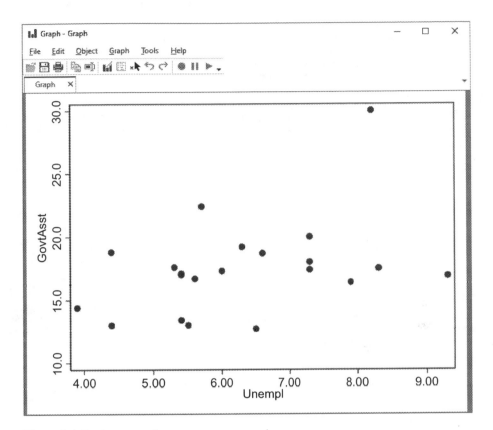

Figure 9.4 Basic output from scatter command

generates the output that we see in Figure 9.5 here. As you might imagine, we can also use the "correlate" command to generate a table of correlation coefficients between any two or more continuous variables.[3] To generate a correlation coefficient with the associated p-value, the syntax is

```
pwcorr variable1 variable2, sig
```

where the command "pwcorr" is short for "pairwise correlations" and can be used to obtain the correlation coefficients for two or more pairs of variables. The "sig" option tells Stata that we want the p-value reported underneath each correlation coefficient. So, if we submit the command

```
pwcorr GovtAsst Unempl, sig
```

we will get the output that is displayed in Figure 9.6, which includes the correlation coefficient (0.3888) that we calculate in Chapter 9 of *FSR* together with its associated p-value (0.0815)

---

[3] The "pw" in pwcorr stands for "pairwise." When examining the relationship between two variables, the correlate and pwcorr commands will yield identical results. However, if multiple variables are investigated, the coefficients can be different for reasons having to do with missing data. Also, the two commands have somewhat different options. Type help pwcorr for more information.

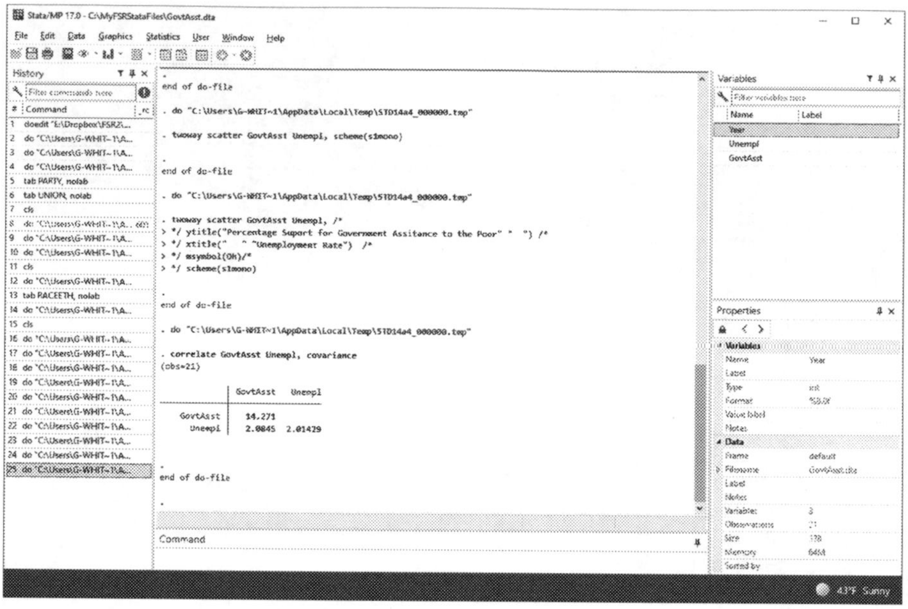

Figure 9.5 Basic output from correlate command with the covariance option

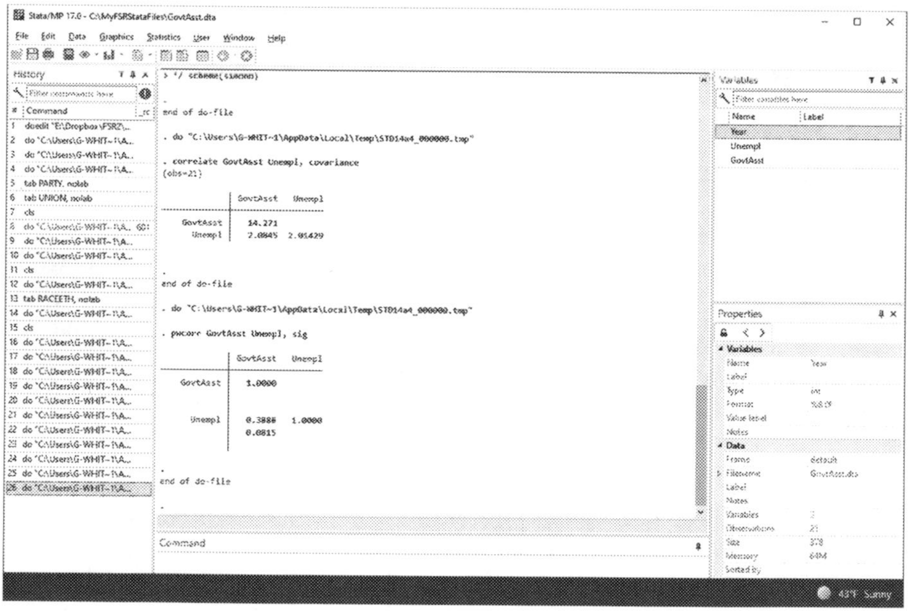

Figure 9.6 Basic output from pwcorr command with the sig option

9.5   ANALYSIS OF VARIANCE

Our final example of bivariate hypothesis testing is analysis of variance, or ANOVA for short. As Table 9.1 in *FSR* shows, ANOVA models, like difference of means tests, require a continuous dependent variable and a

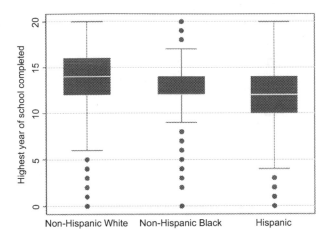

Figure 9.7 Box–whisker plot of racial/ethnic differences in education

categorical independent variable. However, as we discuss in Section 9.4.4 of *FSR*, ANOVA, unlike difference of means tests, is appropriate when the independent variable has three or more, rather than two, categories.

9.5.1 Examining Differences Graphically

As we did earlier in this chapter (Section 9.3) for a continuous dependent variable and an independent variable with two categories, in this section we illustrate how to graphically analyze a continuous dependent variable and an independent variable with three categories. The data set we use is "GSS2014_Chap9_ANOVA.dta." As usual, these data are located in the "MyFSRStataFiles" folder created for this workbook. The command for creating a box–whisker plot for this analysis is

```
graph box EDUC, /*
*/ over(raceeth2, relabel(1 "Non-Hispanic White"
2 "Non-Hispanic Black" 3 "Hispanic")) /*
*/ ytitle("Highest year of school completed" " ")
scheme(s1mono)
```

This command produces the plot displayed in Figure 9.7.

9.5.2 Generating ANOVA Test Statistics

To generate the relevant descriptive statistics for the ANOVA test, we can use the following command:

```
bysort raceeth2: summarize EDUC
```

This command produces the output displayed in the lower-left corner of Figure 9.8.

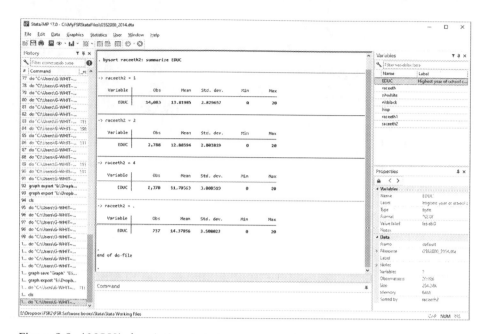

Figure 9.8 ANOVA descriptive statistics

From the descriptive statistics displayed in Figure 9.8, we can see the average number of years of education completed for each group. Are these means large enough to warrant rejection of our null hypothesis of no racial/ethnic group differences in educational attainment in the underlying population? To answer this question, we must conduct an ANOVA test.

To conduct an analysis of variance test such as the one discussed in Chapter 9 of *FSR* and to produce the output displayed in Table 9.12 of *FSR*, you can use the following command:

```
anova EDUC raceeth2
```

This command produces the output displayed at the bottom of Figure 9.9. Look at the last column of the first row of ANOVA output where the *p*-value is reported. Since that value is less than 0.05, we can reject the null hypothesis of equality of population means in favor of the alternative hypothesis that at least one mean (or means) is (are) different from at least one other mean (or means). But which ones are different from which others?

In order to answer this important question, we have to take one additional step. In order to do so, we conduct what is referred to as a multiple comparison procedure. The command for this is

```
oneway EDUC raceeth2, scheffe
```

which produces the output displayed in the lower left of Figure 9.10. An examination of this output shows that each of the group means is

Figure 9.9 ANOVA output

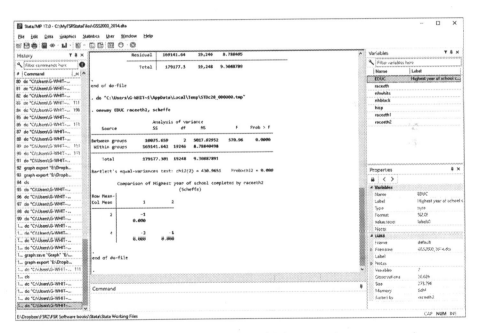

Figure 9.10 Output from a Scheffe ANOVA multiple comparison test procedure

significantly different from each of the other group means. In other words, non-Hispanic whites have significantly higher educational attainment than both non-Hispanic blacks and Hispanics; non-Hispanic blacks have significantly lower educational attainment than non-Hispanic whites but significantly higher educational attainment than Hispanics; and Hispanics are significantly lower on educational attainment than both whites and blacks.

9.6 EXERCISES

1. Launch Stata and load the "GSS2014_Chap9_v5.dta" data set. Once you have done this, conduct a chi-squared test of the null hypothesis that sex and party are statistically independent. Discuss your results.

2. Using the same data set, perform a difference of means test using sex as the independent variable and education as the dependent variable. Discuss your results.

3. Launch Stata and load the "GovtAsst.dta" data set. Once you have done this, output a correlation matrix showing the relationship between unemployment rate and attitudes toward government assistance to the poor. Discuss your results.

4. Launch Stata and load the "GSS2014_Sample_Exercises_Chap9.dta" data set. Perform an analysis of variance to determine whether Protestants, Catholics, and those with no religious affiliation ("Nones") differ on age. If you reject the null hypothesis, perform a multiple comparison procedure to determine which religious groups differ from which others.

10 Two-Variable Regression Models

10.1 OVERVIEW

In Chapter 10 of *FSR* we introduce the two-variable regression model. As we discuss, this is another two-variable hypothesis test that amounts to fitting a line through a scatter plot of observations on a dependent variable and an independent variable. In this chapter, we walk you through how to estimate such a bivariate model in Stata.

10.2 ESTIMATING A TWO-VARIABLE REGRESSION

The estimation of a two-variable regression model, as discussed in Chapter 10 of *FSR*, is fairly straightforward. The syntax is

`regress depvariable indvariable`

where "`regress`" is the command which tells Stata to estimate a regression model, "`depvariable`" is the name of the dependent variable, and "`indvariable`" is the name of the independent variable. This will produce output such as that pictured in Figure 10.4 of *FSR*. In that example, the command, which appears in the top of the figure, was

`reg GovtAsst Unempl`

where "`reg`" is a shortened version of the "`regress`" command which told Stata to estimate a two-variable regression with "`GovtAsst`" as the dependent variable, and "`Unempl`" as the independent variable.

10.3 GRAPHING A TWO-VARIABLE REGRESSION

To better understand what is going on in a two-variable regression model, it is often helpful to graph the regression line. An example of this is presented in Figure 10.3 of *FSR*. The code for producing that figure is:

```
twoway (scatter GovtAsst Unempl) /*
*/ (lfit GovtAsst Unempl, lcolor(black)), /*
*/ ytitle("Percentage Support for Government Assistance to
the Poor") /*
*/ xtitle("Unemployment Rate") /*
*/ legend(off) /*
*/ xline(.7635, lcolor(black) lpattern(dash)
lwidth(thin)) /*
*/ yline(51.92569, lcolor(black) lpattern(dash)
lwidth(thin)) /*
*/ scheme(s1mono)
```

There is obviously a lot going on in this command. As we have moved deeper into this book, we have produced increasingly complicated figures. Rather than writing the many lines of code for a figure such as Figure 10.3 of *FSR* all at once, most researchers will start off with a simple figure, and then gradually add additional details.

We will now walk through an example of how to do this using Figure 10.3 of *FSR*. First, we want to have the linear fit of the model as a line in our figure. This can be done in Stata by issuing the following command:

```
twoway lfit depvariable indvariable
```

where "twoway lfit" tells Stata that we want to produce a twoway graph which shows the linear fit of a two-variable regression model. Issuing the following command:

```
twoway lfit GovtAsst Unempl, scheme(s1mono)
```

produces output like what we see in Figure 10.1.

Next, we want to add a scatter plot which shows the location of each of our observations around the regression line. To do this, we now need to tell Stata that we want to have two different types of twoway graphs together in the same figure. This can be done by first writing the command twoway, and then writing the two or more separate twoway commands each within parentheses without the word "twoway" in front of them. So, keeping with our running example,

```
twoway (scatter GovtAsst Unempl) (lfit GovtAsst Unempl),
scheme(s1mono)
```

would tell Stata to produce output like what we see in Figure 10.2 here. This output certainly shows us the main components of the regression

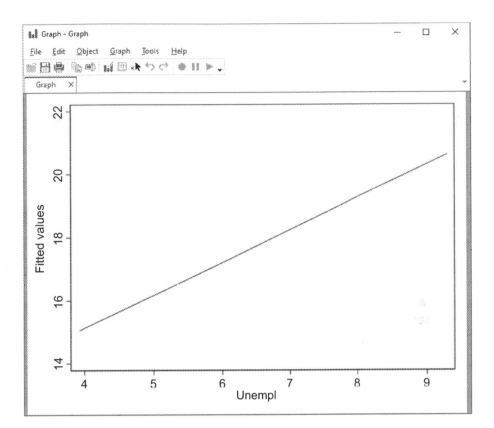

Figure 10.1 Basic output from the twoway lfit command

model, with incumbent vote as the dependent variable and growth as the independent variable.

For Figure 10.3 of *FSR*, we wanted to show that the estimated regression line for a two-variable regression always passes through the intersection of the means of the dependent variable and the independent variable. To get these means, we used the summarize command which we introduced in Chapter 7 of this book. We can then add a vertical line showing the mean of growth with an xline option and a horizontal line showing the mean of vote with a yline option. In both cases, the location on the axis at which we want the line to appear has to be written in parentheses immediately after the option. So, to keep building to our running example,

```
twoway (scatter GovtAsst Unempl) (lfit GovtAsst Unempl), /*
*/ xline(6.285714) yline(17.5) /*
*/ scheme(s1mono)
```

would tell Stata to produce output like what we see in Figure 10.3.

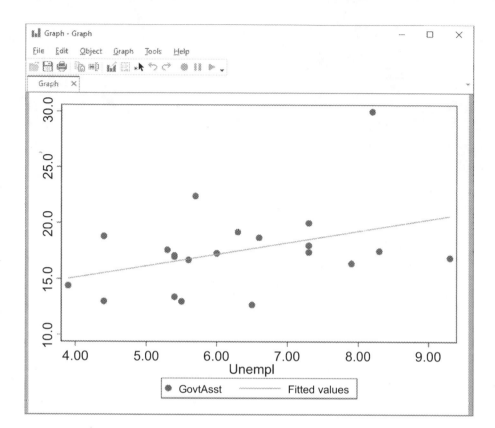

Figure 10.2 Output from the twoway lfit command together with twoway scatter

If we return to the command which produced Figure 10.3 of *FSR*,

```
twoway (scatter GovtAsst Unempl) /*
*/ (lfit GovtAsst Unempl, lcolor(black)), /*
*/ ytitle("Percentage Support for Government Assistance
to the Poor") /*
*/ xtitle("Unemployment Rate") /*
*/ legend(off) /*
*/ xline(.7635, lcolor(black) lpattern(dash)
lwidth(thin)) /*
*/ yline(51.92569, lcolor(black) lpattern(dash)
lwidth(thin)) /*
*/ scheme(s1mono)
```

the remaining parts of the command that we have not discussed in earlier chapters are the following fairly straightforward refinements:

- "lcolor(black)" inside "(lfit, GovtAsst Unempl lcolor (black))" tells Stata that we want the regression line to be drawn in black rather than the grey which we see in Figures 10.1 through 10.3,

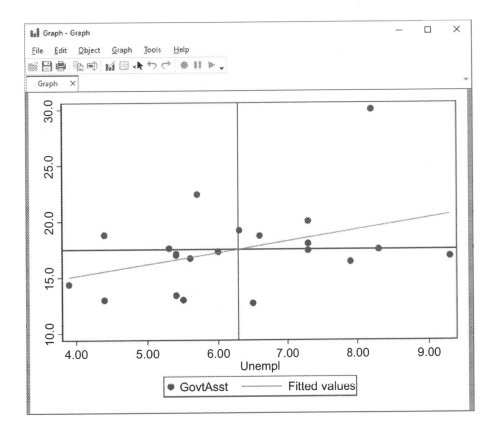

Figure 10.3 Output from the twoway lfit command together with twoway scatter and mean lines

- "legend(off)" tells Stata that we do not want the legend box which appears under Figures 10.2 and 10.3,
- the "lpattern" options tell Stata the pattern that we want for a particular line, and
- the "lwidth" options tell Stata the width that we want for a particular line.

10.4 EXERCISES

1. Open Stata and load the do-file named "Chapter 10 Two-Variable Regression Examples.do" into the do-file editor. Make sure that you have the correct directory path for loading the data. In other words, if "C:\MyFSRStataFiles" is not where you have your data, change this part of the do-file so that the data load into Stata. Once you have done this, run the code to produce Figure 10.3 from *FSR*. Copy and paste this figure into your word processing document.

2. If we change the independent variable in our running example from "unemployment" to "year," what would the theory of economic threat lead us to

expect in terms of a hypothesis for the slope of a regression line with variable "GovtAsst" as the dependent variable and "year" as the independent variable? Explain your answer.

3. Estimate a regression model with the variable "GovtAsst" as the dependent variable and "year" as the independent variable.

   (a) Copy and paste this output into your word processing document.

   (b) Write about the results from the hypothesis test that you discussed above. What does this tell you about the theory of economic threat?

   (c) Produce a figure like Figure 10.3 from *FSR* but with year as the independent variable (GovtAsst should remain as the dependent variable). Copy and paste this figure into your word processing document.

11 Multiple Regression

11.1 OVERVIEW

In Chapter 11 of *FSR*, we introduce the multiple regression model in which we are able to estimate the effect of *X* on *Y* holding *Z* constant. Here, we show you how to execute such models in Stata.

11.2 ESTIMATING A MULTIPLE REGRESSION

The estimation of a multiple regression model, as discussed in Chapter 11 of *FSR*, is just an extension of the command used for estimating a two-variable regression. For example, if we have three independent variables, the syntax is

```
regress depvariable indvariable1 indvariable2 indvariable3
```

where "*depvariable*" is the name of the dependent variable, and the terms that begin with "*indvariable*" are the names of the independent variables.[1] For Stata's multiple regression command, the name of the dependent variable must always come first, followed by the names of the independent variables. The order in which the independent variables appear does not matter; you will get the same results regardless of their order.

The command to estimate the multiple regression displayed under the column titled "C" in Table 10.1 of *FSR* is

```
regress GovtAsst Unempl Degree
```

which produces output like that displayed in Figure 11.1.

---

[1] In this example of the syntax, we have chosen to show the syntax for having three independent variables. In practice, you may have as many independent variables as you want in a regression model as long as you meet the minimum mathematical requirements that each independent variable varies, $n > k$, and you have no perfect multicollinearity. The first two of these requirements are discussed in Section 10.5.3 and the third is discussed in Section 11.8.1 of *FSR*.

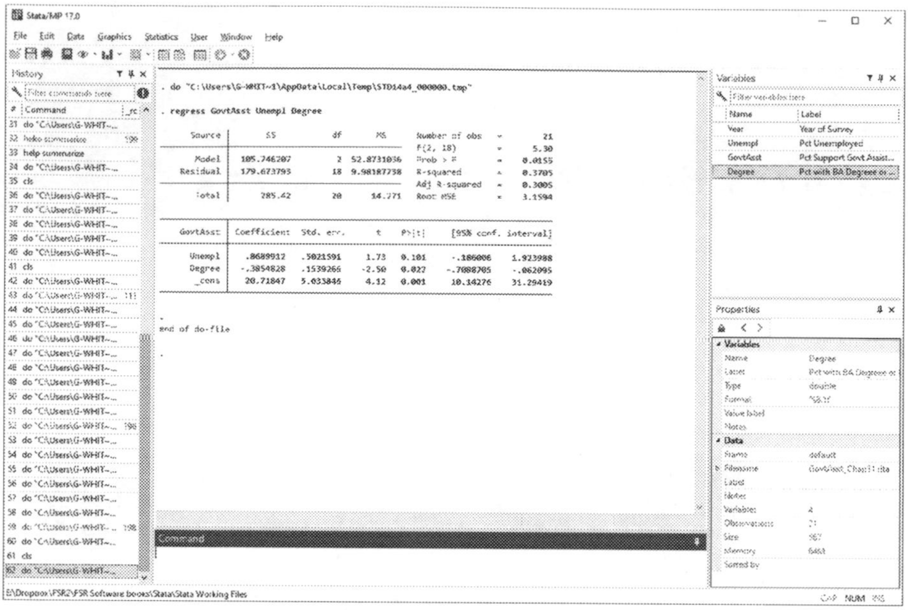

Figure 11.1   Basic output from a multiple regression

11.3   FROM REGRESSION OUTPUT TO TABLE – MAKING ONLY ONE TYPE OF COMPARISON

As we discuss in Section 12.4 of *FSR*, when presenting the results from more than two regression models in the same table, it is important that we set up our comparisons appropriately – either as comparisons of different model specifications estimated with the same sample of data, or as the same model specification estimated with different samples of data. This is because if both the sample of data and the model specification change, then we cannot know for sure whether any differences in the estimates that we are observing are due to the different sample or the different specification.

11.3.1   Comparing Models with the Same Sample of Data, but Different Specifications

If your data set doesn't have any missing values for any of the variables that you want to include in a set of models with different specifications, then making a table for such comparisons is pretty straightforward. All that you need to do is to estimate the regressions of interest to you and put them into separate columns of a table. If, as is often the case, you have some missing values for some of the variables that you are including in your different models, then you need to take some extra steps in order to make sure that the regressions that you are comparing are all estimated with the exact same observations.

As an example of this, let's assume that the variable "Degree" is missing for the year 2010. Since regression models are based on only those cases that have no missing data on any of the variables in the model, it would be necessary for us to exclude the year for which the degree variable was missing. Given that we know the year of the observation that we want to exclude, we can simply tell Stata to select all cases where the value of the variable "year" is not equal to 2010.

One way to do this, given that we know the year of the observation that we want to exclude, would be to write the command as

```
regress GovtAsst Unempl if Year != 2010
```

which tells Stata to estimate a regression with GovtAsst as the dependent variable and Unempl as the independent variable using *only* those observations for which the condition after the `if` statement is met. In this case, this condition is `year != 2010` which translates into "year is not equal to 2010."

But what would we do if we didn't know exactly which observations are missing particular values of particular independent variables?[2] One of the easiest ways is just to estimate the model using all cases that are not missing for any of the independent variables that you plan to include in the models that you want to present. In our running example, we would estimate the following two models:

```
regress GovtAsst Unempl if Degree != .
```

```
regress GovtAsst Degree if Unempl != .
```

where `!= .` in each command translates into "is not equal to missing." These two commands, together with the following command

```
regress GovtAsst Unempl Degree
```

create the output presented in Table 10.1 of *FSR*.

11.3.2 Comparing Models with the Same Specification, but Different Samples of Data

As an example of how to compare models with the same specification, but different samples of data, let's imagine that we want to look at the results

---

[2] If an observation is missing for the dependent variable, it will not be included in any of the models that we estimate. Also, in general, we should have gotten to know our data before we estimate a regression model, and part of getting to know one's data is figuring out what are the missing values and why they are missing.

from our running example of support for government assistance to the poor for observations after the turn of the twenty-first century compared with all observations before then. So, to estimate models on samples of data beginning in 2000 and all other cases, we would estimate the following two models:

```
regress GovtAsst Unempl Degree if Year <2000

regress GovtAsst Unempl Degree if Year >1999
```

where the commands are identical except for the conditions written after the "if."

11.4 STANDARDIZED COEFFICIENTS

In order to obtain standardized coefficients, as discussed in Section 11.6 of *FSR*, you can add a comma and the word "beta" to the multiple regression syntax:

```
regress depvariable indvariable1 indvariable2
indvariable3, beta
```

To estimate such a model with GovtAsst as our dependent variable, and Unempl and Degree as our independent variables,

```
regress GovtAsst Unempl Degree, beta
```

we will get output like that displayed at the bottom of Figure 11.2.

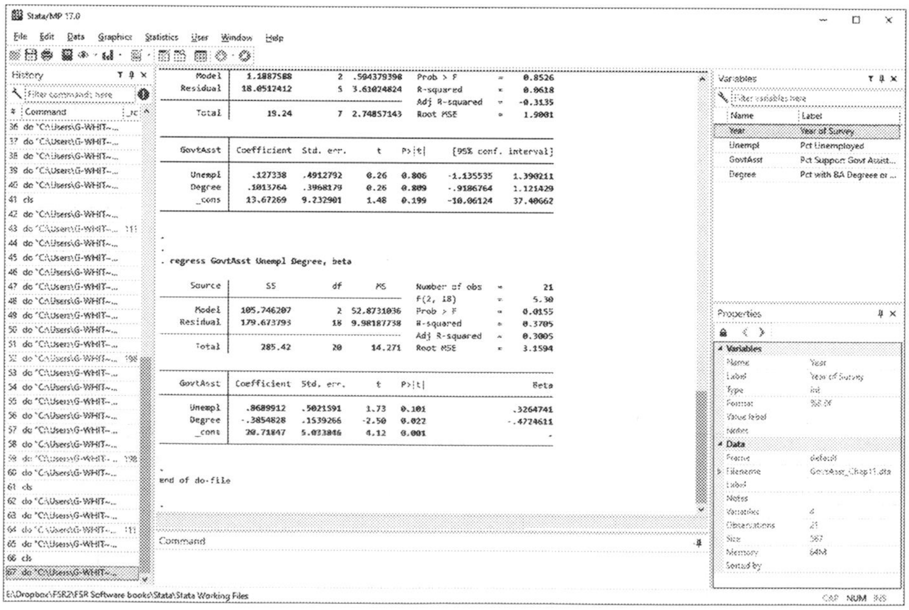

Figure 11.2 Basic output from a multiple regression with the "beta" option

11.5 DUMMY VARIABLES

As we discuss in Section 11.9 of *FSR*, dummy variables are variables that take on one of two different values. The vast majority of the time, these two values are "zero" and "one." Dummy variables are usually created and named so that "one" represents the presence of a condition and "zero" represents the absence of that condition. In order to not confuse the people who will be reading your work or watching your presentations, it is a good idea to follow these conventions. For example, if you have a dummy variable to identify the gender identity of a survey respondent, it might be tempting to call the variable "gender." That, however, would leave unclear the issue of what the zeros and ones represent. If, by contrast, you named your variable "female," then the convention would be that a zero is for male respondents – or the absence of the condition "female" – and one is for the female respondents – the presence of the condition "female."

11.5.1 Creating a Dummy Variable with the "Generate" and "Replace" Commands

Sometimes data sets that you are working with come with proper dummy variables already created for you. When they do not, you will need to create your own variables. There are multiple ways to create dummy variables in Stata. In general, we recommend that you first create a new variable with all of its values set to missing. In Stata, the "generate" command tells Stata that you want to create a new variable and the code for a missing value is a period ".", so the command:

```
generate newvariable=.
```

will create a new variable with all missing values. We can then use the "replace" command to replace the missing values with the appropriate values that we want. For instance, if the dummy variable that we want to create is from an existing variable with values of 7 and 9 which we want to make 1 and 0, respectively, we would use the following syntax:

```
replace newvariable=1 if oldvariable==7
```

```
replace newvariable=0 if oldvariable==9
```

which tells Stata to replace the missing values in *newvariable* with 1 if the *oldvariable* was equal to 7 and to replace the missing values in *newvariable* with 0 if the *oldvariable* was equal to 9. Stata reads the "==" in the two commands above as "is exactly equal to."[3]

---

[3] As is often the case, there are many different ways to create new variables in Stata. One more succinct way to adjust the values of a new variable that you create is to use the recode command. This command allows you to change all of the values of a new variable

Whenever you create a new variable, it is critically important to check that you created exactly what you intended to create. One way to check this is with a `tab2` command which we introduced in Section 9.2. In this case, we could check our work with the command:

```
tab2 oldvariable newvariable
```

which tells Stata to create a two-variable table with the nonmissing values of *newvariable* and *oldvariable*.

So, to create the data for the example in Section 11.9 of *FSR*, we first load the Stata data set named "GSS2016_Sample_Chap11.dta," which is a subset of the 2016 GSS. From the codebook for this study, we can tell that coding of values for each respondent's self-identified gender is in the variable named "SEX" and that the values of this variable are equal to 1 for "male" and 2 for "female." To check the values for this variable, we submit the command:

```
tab SEX, missing
```

Having seen that there are only values equal to 1 and 2, we can now create the variable "female" and check what we have created using the following commands:

```
generate female=.
replace female=0 if SEX==1
replace female=1 if SEX==2
tab2 SEX female, missing
```

The output from these commands is displayed in Figure 11.3.

11.5.2 Estimating a Multiple Regression Model with a Single Dummy Independent Variable

As we discussed in Section 11.2 of this software companion book, the syntax for estimating a multiple regression with three independent variables is:

```
regress depvariable indvariable1 indvariable2 indvariable3
```

where "*depvariable*" is the name of the dependent variable, and the "*indvariable*" terms are the names of the three independent variables. When we have only a single dummy independent variable, then we just simply add the name of that variable to the list after "*depvariable*."

---

in a single line of code. While this is a quicker way to get things done, we have found that new users often make more mistakes when using the `recode` than they do when they use the `replace` command and make one change per line of code.

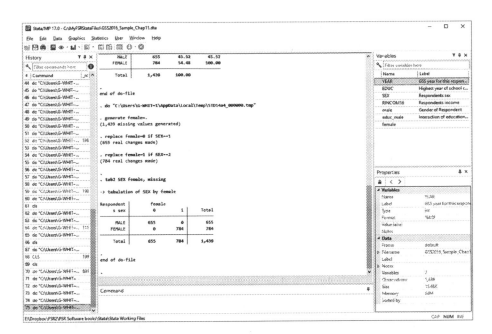

Figure 11.3 Output from creating a dummy variable

As an example of this, we can estimate the regression model displayed on the left side of Table 11.1 of *FSR* with the following command:

```
regress RINCOM16 female EDUC
```

where "RINCOM16" is the dependent variable (respondents' income), "income" is a continuous independent variable, and "female" is the dummy independent variable that we just created. Note that, as was the case with our multiple regression models with multiple continuous independent variables, the order of the independent variables does not matter for this command. The output from this command is displayed in Figure 11.4.

11.5.3 Estimating a Multiple Regression Model with Multiple Dummy Independent Variables

To estimate a multiple regression model with multiple dummy variables, you use the same command syntax as in the previous section. The main complication comes when the multiple dummy variables represent values for a categorical variable with more than two values. As we discuss in Section 11.9.1 of *FSR*, in such a case, in order to avoid what is known as the "dummy variable trap," you need to leave one category of such an independent variable out of the regression model, and that left-out category becomes the "reference category."

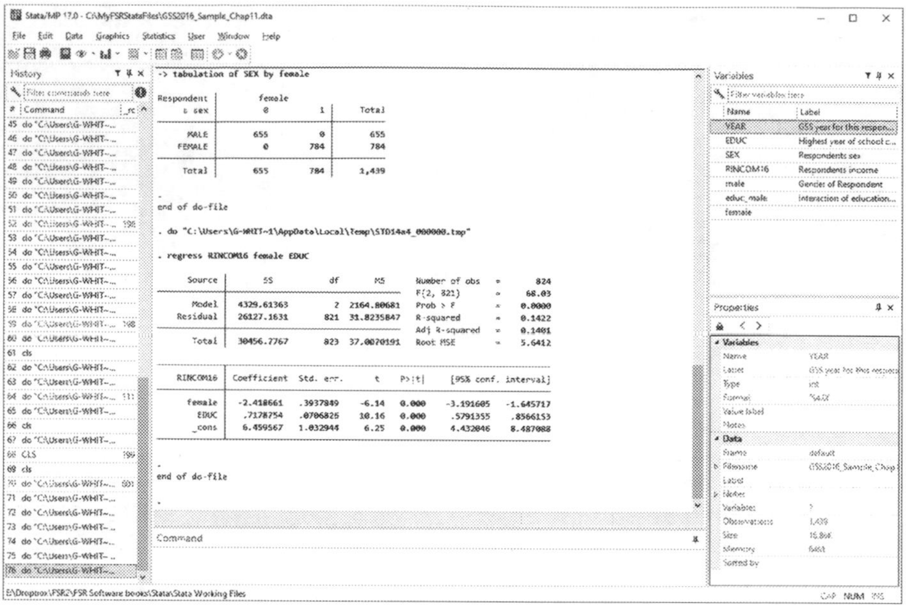

Figure 11.4 Output from a regression model with a dummy variable

11.6   DUMMY VARIABLES IN INTERACTIONS

In Section 11.10 of *FSR*, we discuss testing interactive hypotheses with dummy variables. There are several different ways to do this in Stata. We recommend that you use a fairly straightforward approach where you start out by creating a new variable that is the multiplicative interaction between the dummy independent variable and the continuous independent variable. The syntax for creating a new variable that is the product of two variables already in the data set is

```
generate newvariable=oldvariable1*oldvariable2
```

where *newvariable* is the name of the interaction, *oldvariable1* and *oldvariable2* are the names of the dummy variable and the continuous variable that you wish to interact (the order of them does not matter), and "*" tells Stata to multiply the values of these two variables.

To estimate a multiple regression with this interaction, you would use the following syntax:

```
regress depvariable newvariable oldvariable1 oldvariable2
```

which could also include more independent variables in addition to *oldvariable1* and *oldvariable2*. As with all multiple regressions, the order of the independent variables in such a command line does not matter.

In order to create the interactive model displayed on the right side of Table 11.9 of *FSR*, we first create the interaction between the continuous variable EDUC and the dummy variable male with the following code:

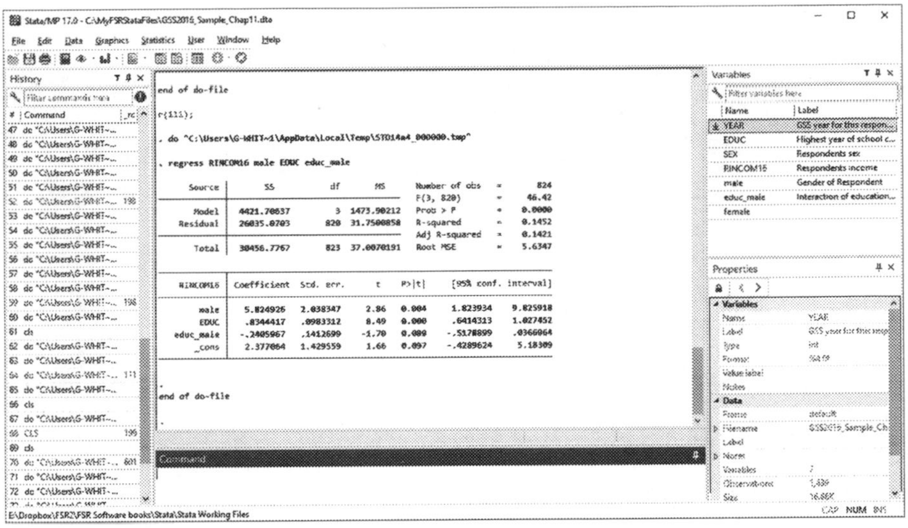

Figure 11.5 Output from a regression model with an interaction

```
generate educ_male = EDUC*male
```

We can then run the following command to produce the desired regression output:

```
regress RINCOM16 male EDUC educ_male
```

The output from this command is displayed in Figure 11.5.

11.7 MODELS WITH DUMMY DEPENDENT VARIABLES

As we discuss in Chapter 11 of *FSR*, there are several different models that can be used when we have a dummy dependent variable. In this set of examples, we will work with data from the 2004 American National Election Study (ANES) with a dependent variable named "Bush," which equals 1 for respondents who reported that they voted for George W. Bush and equals 0 for those respondents who reported that they voted for John Kerry.[4] To get a look at the values for this variable, we can run a tab command

```
tab Bush
```

which produces the output displayed in Figure 11.6.

As we discuss in Chapter 11 of *FSR*, one option when we have a limited dependent variable is simply to run a regression model using the

---

[4] This is the same example that we use in Chapter 11 of *FSR*. For a more detailed explanation of the variable and how it was created, see the footnote at the beginning of Section 11.11.1 of *FSR*.

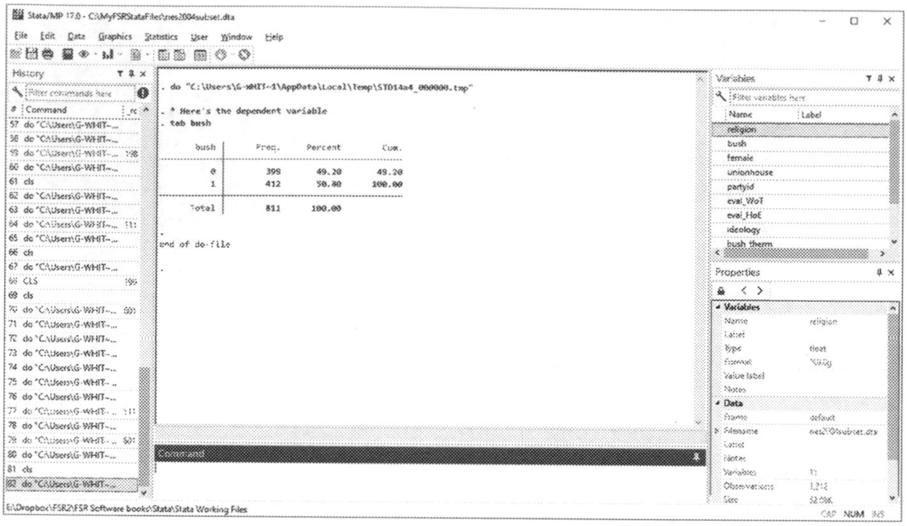

Figure 11.6 Table of values for the variable "Bush"

standard syntax that we discussed in this companion book. For example, if we have three independent variables, the syntax is

```
regress depvariable indvariable1 indvariable2 indvariable3
```

and the only difference is that the *depvariable* is a dummy variable. So, if we want to estimate the model displayed in Table 11.10 of *FSR*, we would write the command as

```
regress bush partyid eval_WoT eval_HoE
```

where "bush" is the dependent variable for which the values are displayed in Figure 11.6, "partyid" is "Party Identification," "eval_WoT" is "Evaluation: War on Terror," and "eval_HoE" is "Evaluation: Health of the Economy."

To calculate and summarize the predicted probabilities from this model, we use the following commands with what should now be familiar syntax

```
predict yhat, xb
```

```
summarize yhat, detail
```

which produces the output displayed in Figure 11.7.[5] Looking at this output, we can see that, when we create the new variable named "yhat," Stata gives us a message about missing values being generated. This is the case because Stata will only calculate the predicted values for those cases

---

[5] The option "xb" tells Stata that we want the predicted values from a linear regression model that we are calling "yhat."

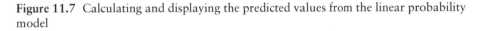

Figure 11.7 Calculating and displaying the predicted values from the linear probability model

that were included in the regression model that we just estimated. If we look at the results from the summarize command, we can see that we get some predicted values (what we refer to as $\hat{P}_i$ values) that are greater than 1. As we discuss in Chapter 11 of *FSR*, one of the problems of the linear probability model is that it can produce predicted probabilities that are greater than 1 or less than 0. This is one of the main reasons why some researchers prefer to use either a binomial logit (BNL) model or a binomial probit (BNP) model when they have a dummy dependent variable.

To estimate a binomial logit model in Stata, the syntax is

```
logit depvariable indvariable1 indvariable2 indvariable3
```

and to estimate a binomial probit model in Stata, the syntax is

```
probit depvariable indvariable1 indvariable2 indvariable3
```

As we discuss in Chapter 11 of *FSR*, with each of these types of models there is an estimated systematic component for each observation, what we call the $X_i \hat{\beta}$ values, that can be put through a link function to produce predicted probabilities, what we refer to as $\hat{P}_i$ values. The command for calculating the $\hat{P}_i$ values after either a binomial logit or binomial probit has been estimated is

```
predict newvariable, pr
```

where "newvariable" is the name of the new variable that we want to create, and the "pr" option tells Stata that we want the new variable to be the predicted probabilities for each of our observations that were included in the regression estimation.

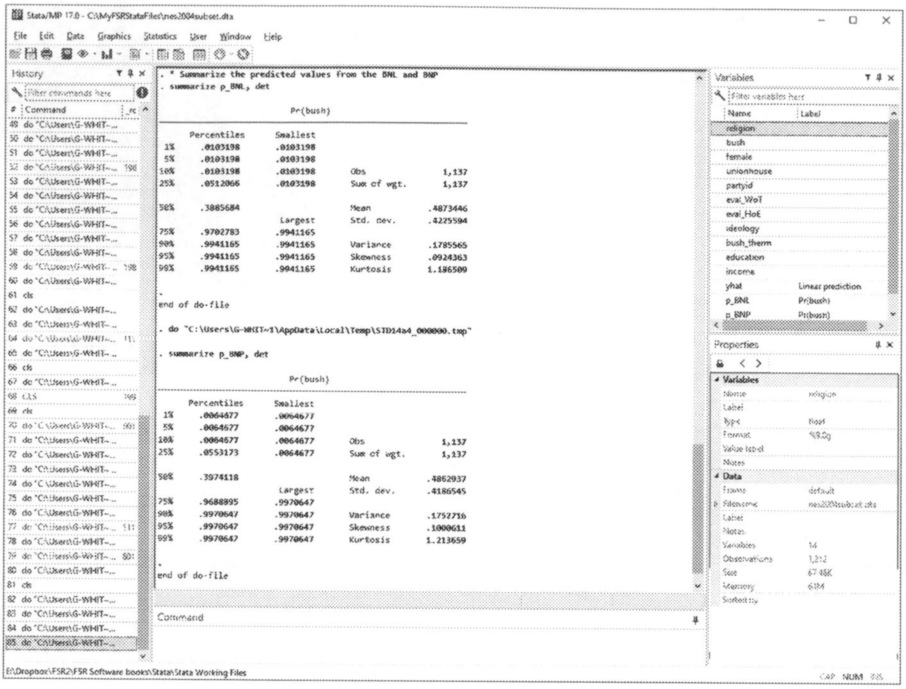

Figure 11.8 Summary statistics for predicted values from a binomial logit model and a binomial probit model

So, to continue with our running example, we can produce the logit and probit columns of the results displayed in Table 11.11 of *FSR* and predicted probabilities for each observation by running the following lines of code:

```
logit bush partyid eval_WoT eval_HoE predict p_BNL, pr

probit bush partyid eval_WoT eval_HoE predict p_BNP, pr
```

We can then display summary statistics for the resulting predicted probabilities by running the following lines of code:

```
summarize p_BNL, det

summarize p_BNP, det
```

which produces the output presented in Figure 11.8.

In order to produce classification tables like Table 11.12 in *FSR*, we need to first create a new variable, which is the predicted value of the dependent variable, what we have labeled "Model-based expectations" in Table 11.12 in *FSR*. For the linear probability model in this example, we would use the following three lines of code:

```
gen p_vote_LPM=yhat
recode p_vote_LPM -.1/.5=0 .5000001/1.2=1
tab2 bush p_vote_LPM, cell
```

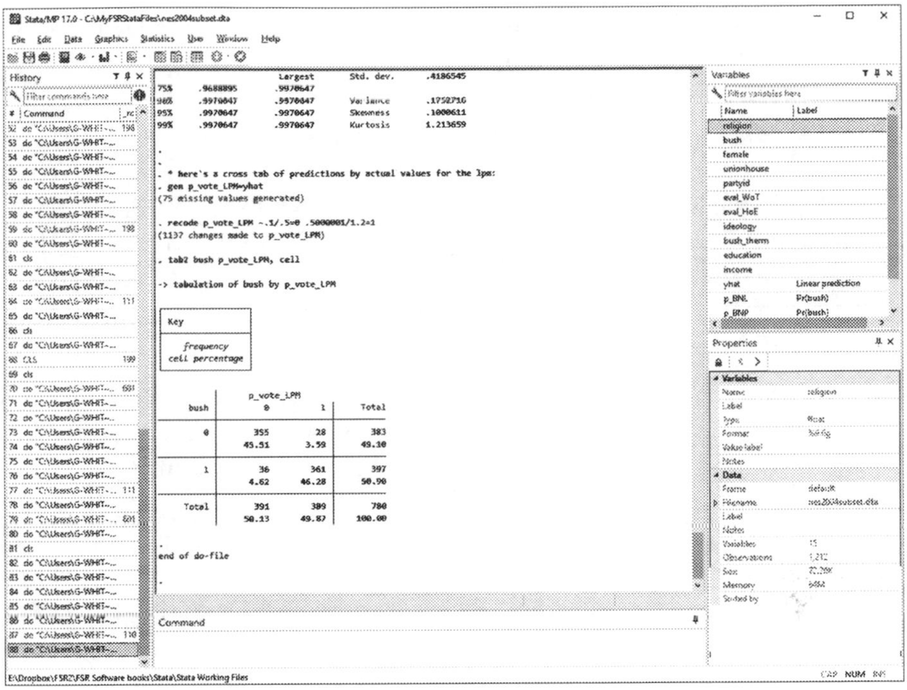

Figure 11.9 Raw output used to produce Table 11.12 of *FSR*

where we first create a new variable p_vote_LPM equal to the predicted values from the linear probability model that we estimated. We then recode the values of p_vote_LPM so that predicted probabilities of 0.5 or smaller become predictions that the individual will vote for Kerry (coded as 0) and predicted probabilities greater than 0.5 become predictions that the individual will vote for Bush (coded as 1). We then produce a table of the values of actual vote and our model-based predictions. The output from these commands is presented in Figure 11.9.

11.8 EXERCISES

1. Open the do-file named "Chapter 11 Multiple Regression Examples.do" in Stata. Make sure that you have the correct directory path for loading the data. In other words, if "C:\MyFSRStataFiles" is not where you have your data, change this part of the script file so that the data load into Stata. Once you have done this, run the code to produce the output shown in Figure 11.1. Copy and paste this figure into your word processing document.

2. Estimate the two multiple regression models described in this chapter with the same specification but where the sample is divided according to whether the observation occurred before or after 2000. Put these results into a table in your word processing document and write about what you have found.

3. Estimate a multiple regression model with standardized coefficients. Put your results into a table in your word processing document and write about what you have found.

4. Open the do-file named "Chapter 11 Dummy Dependent Variable Examples.do" in Stata. Make sure that you have the correct directory path for loading the data. In other words, if "C:\MyFSRStataFiles" is not where you have your data, change this part of the script file so that the data load into Stata. Once you have done this, run the code to produce the results presented in Table 11.11 of *FSR*. Copy and paste this figure into your word processing document.

5. Using the code at the bottom of "Chapter 11 Dummy Dependent Variable Examples.do," create a classification table for the BNL and the BNP models. Copy and paste this into your word processing document.

6. Calculate the proportionate reduction in error from a naive model to the BNL and from a naive model to the BNP. Write briefly about what you have learned from doing this.

12 Putting It All Together to Produce Effective Research

12.1 OVERVIEW

In Chapter 12 of *FSR*, we tie the broad lessons of the book together in order to help you on your way to producing compelling research. In the last chapter of this companion book, we have some exercises for you to get you moving in this direction.

12.2 EXERCISES

1. Launch Stata and load the "GSS2016_Sample_Chap12.dta" data set. Once you have done this, you'll see that there are five variables in this subsample from the 2016 GSS: YEAR (2016 only), EDUC (highest year of schooling completed), SEX (male or female), RINCOM16 (respondent's income in 2016), and RACE (non-Hispanic whites and non-Hispanics blacks only). RINCOM16 will be the dependent variable in the exercises for this chapter. Run the commands necessary to output appropriate descriptive statistics for the dependent variable (including a box–whisker plot) and write a brief summary of what you have found. Copy and paste the box–whisker plot into your word processing document.

2. Estimate a two-variable regression model with RINCOM16 as the dependent variable and EDUC as the independent variable. Write about what you have found. Copy and paste the output into your word processing document.

3. Estimate a multiple regression model with EDUC, SEX (coded 1 for females and 0 for males), and RACE (coded 1 for non-Hispanic blacks and 0 for non-Hispanic whites) as independent variables, and RINCOM16 as the dependent variable. Put your results into a table in your word processing document and write about what you have found.

4. Estimate the same multiple regression model as above but reverse the coding of both dummy variables so that males are coded 1 and females are coded 0, and non-Hispanic whites are coded 1 and non-Hispanic blacks are coded 0. Put

these results into a table in your word processing document and write about what you have found.

5. Estimate a multiple regression model with standardized coefficients with EDUC and the dummy variables for SEX and RACE as the independent variables, and RINCOM16 as the dependent variable. Put your results into a table in your word processing document and write about what you have found.

6. Create an interaction term between the dummy variables that you created for female and non-Hispanic black respondents. Then estimate a multiple regression model with education, the dummy variables for females and non-Hispanic blacks, and the interaction term as the independent variables, and RINCOM16 as the dependent variable. Write a brief summary of what these results tell you.

References

Bansak, Kirk, Jens Hainmueller, and Dominik Hangartner. 2016. "How Economic, Humanitarian, and Religious Concerns Shape European Attitudes Toward Asylum Seekers." *Science* 354(6309):217–222.

Branton, Regina P., and Bradford S. Jones. 2005. "Reexamining Racial Attitudes: The Conditional Relationship Between Diversity and Socioeconomic Environment." *American Journal of Political Science* 49(2):359–372.

Esses, Victoria M., John F. Dovidio, Lynne M. Jackson, and Tamara L. Armstrong. 2001. "The Immigration Dilemma: The Role of Perceived Group Competition, Ethnic Prejudice, and National Identity." *Journal of Social Issues* 57(3):389–412.

King, Gary, Benjamin Schneer, and Ariel White. 2017. "How the News Media Activate Public Expression and Influence National Agendas." *Science* 358(6364): 776–780.

McLaren, Lauren M. 2003. "Anti-Immigrant Prejudice in Europe: Contact, Threat Perception, and Preferences for the Exclusion of Migrants." *Social Forces* 81(3):909–936.

Perry, Samuel L., Ryon J. Cobb, Andrew L. Whitehead, and Joshua B. Grubbs. 2021. "Divided by Faith (in Christian America): Christian Nationalism, Race, and Divergent Perceptions of Racial Injustice." *Social Forces*, soab134, https://doi.org/10.1093/sf/soab134.

Scarborough, William J., Joanna R. Pepin, Danny L. Lambouths III, Ronald Kwon, and Ronaldo Monasterio. 2021. "The Intersection of Racial and Gender Attitudes, 1977 Through 2018." *American Sociological Review* 86(5):823–855.

Sullivan, Jas M., and Alexandra Ghara. 2015. "Racial Identity and Intergroup Attitudes: A Multiracial Youth Analysis." *Social Science Quarterly* 96(1):261–272.

Index

Excel, 38–44

files
   locating, 7
   opening, 4–8
frequency tables, 30–33

General Social Survey (GSS), 8
"generate" command, 67–68
Google, 15
Google Scholar, 15–18
graphics schemes, 14
graphs *see* charts and graphs

histograms, 35–36
hypothesis testing *see* bivariate hypothesis
   testing

independent variables
   in bivariate hypothesis tests, 45–48, 53
   dummy variables, 68–70
   in multiple regression, 63, 68–70
   in two-variable regression, 57
interactive models, with dummy
   variables, 70–71

kernel density plots, 35–36

labels/legends, 13–14, 33, 35
linear probability model (LPM), 73–75
link function, 73
literature searching, 15–19
   exercises, 19

Mac computers, 2
mean value, 41–43
measurement, exercises, 27–29
missing values, 64–65
moment statistics, 35
multiple comparison procedures, 54–56
multiple regression
   constructing regression tables, 64–66
   creating dummy variables, 67–70
   dummy dependent variables, 71–75
   dummy independent variables, 68–70
   estimating, 63–64, 68–70
   exercises, 75
   interactive models with dummy
      variables, 70–71
   standardized coefficients, 66
"My Library" in Google Scholar, 16, 17

opening files, 4–8
ordinal variables, 30–33

p-values, 47, 54, 73
pairwise correlations (pwcorr), 51
pie graphs, 31–32
presentation of tables and graphs,
   36–37
probability, dice rolling in Excel, 38–44
pull-down menus, 4–6

rank statistics, 35
reference category, 69–70
regression lines, graphing, 58–61
regression tables, constructing, 64–66
"replace" command, 67–68
research
   examining previous research, 15
   project exercises, 77–78
research designs, exercises, 23–25

scatter plots, 50, 51, 58–61
standardized coefficients, 66
STATA
   command lines, 14
   command methods, 3–8
   examining data in, 8–9
   launching, 3
   platforms, 2
   versions of, 3
STATA exercises
   basics, 10
   bivariate hypothesis testing, 56
   charts and graphs, 19, 37
   descriptive statistics, 37
   multiple regression, 75–76
   producing research projects, 77–78
   two-variable regression, 61–62
statistical description *see* descriptive
   statistics
statistical moments, 35
statistical output, presentation of, 36–37
summary statistics, 33–36
survey research, exercises, 26

t-test, 49
tables
   covariance tables, 50–52
   frequency tables, 30–33

Printed in the United States
by Baker & Taylor Publisher Services